THE

365 DAY

DEVOTIONAL FOR

SINGERS AND MUSICIANS

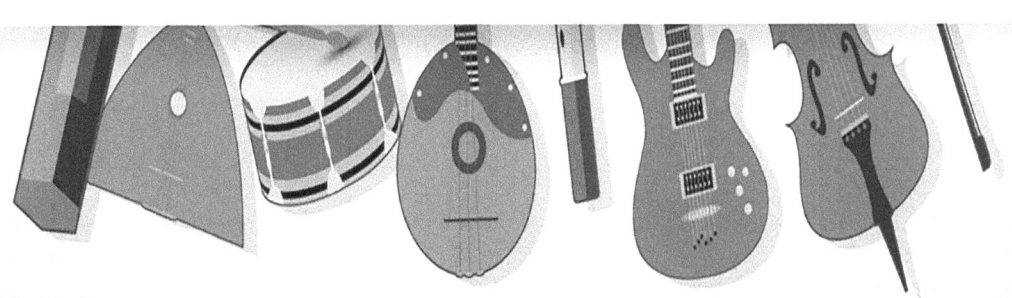

THE
365 DAY
DEVOTIONAL FOR
SINGERS AND MUSICIANS
KEVIN STOUT

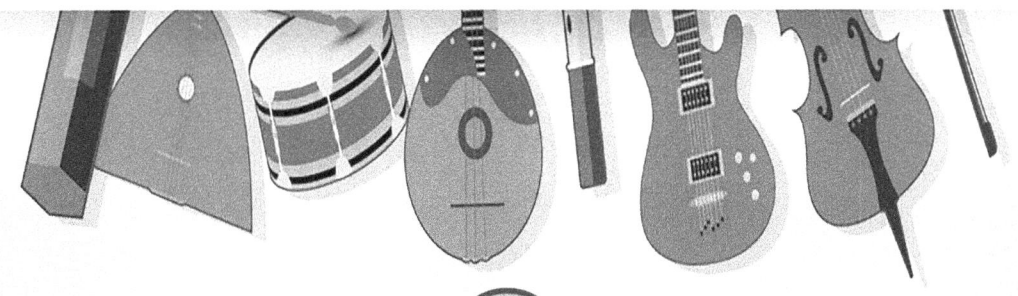

ARPress
ILLUMINATING IDEAS
EMPOWERING VOICES

ARPress
45 Dan Road Suite 5
Canton MA 02021
Hotline: 1(888) 821-0229
Fax: 1(508) 545-7580

Ordering Information:

Quantity sales. Special discounts are available on quantity purchases by corporations, associations, and others. For details, contact the publisher at the address above.

Printed in the United States of America.

ISBN-13:	Softcover	979-8-89330-758-0
	eBook	979-8-89330-760-3
	Hardback	979-8-89330-759-7

Library of Congress Control Number: 2024903485

January 1

> Then Israel sang this song: "Spring up, O
> well! *Sing* about it." (Numbers 21:17; emphasis
> mine)

What a great way to start the day! Sing, especially when you can sing to the Lord, "Spring up, O Well," within my soul. In John 4, Jesus shares with a Samaritan woman that anyone who accepts the water He offers will never thirst again. Even though the world says you need what it has to offer, Jesus says He is all we need. Amen! Sing!

January 2

> Hear this, you kings! Listen, you rulers! I,
> even I, will *sing* to the lord; I will praise the lord,
> the God of Israel, in song. (Judges 5:3; emphasis
> mine)

From "The Song of Deborah," national victories were celebrated by singing. How about you? Has the Lord done battle for you and won? Can you celebrate what the Lord has provided for you? Sing and make music for the Lord today. Let everyone in your world (house, room, office, garage), your nation hear you sing.

January 3

> For the director of music. A psalm of
> David. The heavens declare the glory of God;
> the skies proclaim the work of his hands. (Psalm
> 19:1)

One great thing about the heavens and the sky is that we have to look up to see them. Jesus looked up when he prayed (see John 17:1), and we can as well. It is incredible to think that the God who created the heavens and the earth wants to be praised by you. Sing to Him!

January 4

> My lips will shout for joy when I *sing* praise to you—I whom you have delivered. (Psalm 71:23; emphasis mine)

Sing loud! How would you feel if your child came up to you and shouted while singing, "I love you!" Our Father in heaven feels the same way. Unconditional love has an incredible feeling! As believers, we have been delivered from the enemy, freed from the chains of sin. When He looks at you through the blood of Jesus, He sees you spotless! Sing praise to Him!

January 5

> The priests, the Levites, the gatekeepers, the *musicians* and the temple servants, along with certain of the people and the rest of the Israelites, settled in their own towns. [*Ezra Reads the Law*] When the seventh month came and the Israelites had settled in their towns. (Nehemiah 7:73; emphasis mine)

What a privilege to have an assignment as a musician. God has identified a certain group of people that He has blessed with gifts and talents of creating and playing music. Our worship is so much better because of music. Our relationship is better because of what He has blessed us with.

January 6

> For the director of *music*. To the tune of "Lilies." Of the Sons of Korah. A maskil. A wedding song. My heart is stirred by a noble theme as I recite my verses for the king; my tongue is the pen of a skillful writer. (Psalm 45:1; emphasis mine)

Don't you just love it when God touches your heart with scripture? I have no idea of what the tune of "Lilies" sounds like, but I bet we get to hear it in heaven. Think about scripture as a wedding song, and you are part of the church, the bride of Christ. Ever write something for God? Sing it!

January 7

> Now when you hear the sound of the horn, flute, zither, lyre, harp, pipe and all kinds of *music*, if you are ready to fall down and worship the image I made, very good. But if you do not worship it, you will be thrown immediately into a blazing furnace. Then what god will be able to rescue you from my hand? (Daniel 3:15; emphasis mine)

Be careful, little ears, what you hear! Let's make sure that the music we listen to does not cause us to bow in worship to an idol or a god that is not *the* God. There are lots of gods competing for your allegiance: money, material things, alcohol, beauty, media, etc. Good music can enhance the attraction to these things. Praise God today for all the musicians you know!

January 8

> *Sing* the praises of the lord, you his faithful people; praise his holy name. (Psalm 30:4; emphasis mine)

Open your mouth. Say, "Ahhh." Remember getting medicine that way as a kid? Singing is great medicine for your spirit! In heaven, I bet there is not a single soul who just listens. Go ahead, open up My heart laments for Moab like a harp, my and sing! It will make you feel better.

January 9

> Asaph was the chief, and next to him in rank were Zechariah, then Jaaziel, Shemiramoth,

Jehiel, Mattithiah, Eliab, Benaiah, Obed-Edom and Jeiel. They were to play the lyres and *harps*, Asaph was to sound the cymbals. (1 Chronicles 16:5; emphasis mine)

Kind of makes me wonder if Asaph was a drummer, since he played with cymbals. (Drummers will like this.) So Asaph is the chief, and the rest are listed by rank. So the string players (guitarists) are lower in rank than the drummers. Praise God today for the drummers you know.

January 10

The king used the almugwood to make supports for the temple of the lord and for the royal palace, and to make harps and lyres for the *musicians*. So much almugwood has never been imported or seen since that day. (1 Kings 10:12; emphasis mine)

Research suggests that almugwood is like a red sandalwood—incredibly beautiful, extraordinarily strong and smells good. I remember sandalwood from my incense days. I would love to hear what a twelve string would sound like with almugwood as part of the composition of materials. I bet the king liked the sound!

January 11

My heart laments for Moab like a *harp*, my inmost being for Kir Hareseth. (Isaiah 16:11; emphasis mine)

It is amazing what happens to a major chord when you change it to a minor chord. When played, the chord changes from happy to sad. I have to think that the chord progression that the Lord or Isaiah was thinking of was very sad. The power of music to influence our hearts is unmistakable.

January 12

Sing to the lord a new song, for he has done marvelous things; his right hand and his holy arm have worked salvation for him. (Psalm 98:1; emphasis mine)

Most songs are thoughts expressed in a more organized way than just making notes or jotting an idea down. Many thoughts and ideas written down are turned into song simply by applying those words to a melody that is familiar to you. Let me encourage you to sing a new song to the Lord, one with your own words. Sing it to Him and then maybe to the rest of us.

January 13

When a *trumpet* blast is sounded, the tribes camping on the east are to set out. (Numbers 10:5; emphasis mine)

Doesn't that just want to make you go out and buy an alarm clock that blows a trumpet blast instead of that annoying *beep, beep, beep*? Anyway, music puts us in motion! God uses the trumpet more than any other instrument in Scripture to signal significant events.

January 14

Make *music* to the lord with the harp, with the harp and the sound of singing. (Psalm 98:5; emphasis mine)

Pick up your guitar and play it for the Lord. Sing while you are playing. The Lord loves to hear you play music. I love to hear my granddaughter play on the piano and sing while she plays. It does not matter that she does not know any chords or songs. I love to hear her be creative. Go ahead, be a kid and play for the Lord!

January 15

Besides their 7,337 male and female slaves; and they also had 200 male and female *singers*. (Ezra 2:65; emphasis mine)

A two-hundred-voice choir! There is something special about singing with others as a duet, a trio, a quartet, or any size group. Hearing the blend of voices is just beautiful, the harmony that can be created by augmenting the melody line with tones higher and lower. Imagine what the harmonies in heaven will sound like!

January 16

> And you will *sing* as on the night you celebrate a holy festival; your hearts will rejoice as when people playing pipes go up to the mountain of the lord, to the Rock of Israel. (Isaiah 30:29; emphasis mine)

So what will you do when the Lord comes back? You will sing! If you are a musician, you will play! If you are a singer, you will sing! Your focus will be on the Lord. Today is a great day to practice worshipping our heavenly Father through music!

January 17

> This is what the lord says: "*Sing* with joy for Jacob; shout for the foremost of the nations. Make your praises heard, and say, 'lord, save your people, the remnant of Israel.'" (Jeremiah 31:7; emphasis mine)

Regardless of anything that has happened, or not happened, Israel is still God's chosen nation. Sing *with* joy, not just singing but singing unselfishly for the nation that God says is His chosen people. You are an ingrafted branch of that vine. Rejoice and sing!

January 18

> Let his faithful people rejoice in this honor and *sing* for joy on their beds. (Psalm 149:5; emphasis mine)

Here is a bit of encouragement for you today: be faithful! The faithful are those who are steadfast in allegiance, those who are loyal. No wonder they felt like singing!

January 19

> The seven priests carrying the seven
> *trumpets* went forward, marching before the ark
> of the lord and blowing the *trumpets*. The armed
> men went ahead of them and the rear guard
> followed the ark of the lord, while the *trumpets*
> kept sounding. (Joshua 6:13; emphasis mine)

I think that the trumpet in Joshua's day was like the *instant messaging* of our day. The sound of the trumpet let everyone know that something was happening. God could have just said, "Hey, Jericho! A week from now, you are going to have an awfully bad day." Instead, He chose a musical instrument as the signal for all to shout, and then the walls came down.

January 20

> The king used the algumwood to make
> steps for the temple of the lord and for the royal
> palace, and to make harps and lyres for the
> *musicians*. Nothing like them had ever been seen
> in Judah.) (2 Chronicles 9:11; emphasis mine)

It really is amazing to hear what a difference the wood makes in the sound of stringed instruments. Today, many guitar manufacturers are extremely versatile in the selection and use of different woods for the tops, sides, and backs of guitars.

January 21

> So, Joab blew the *trumpet*, and all the
> troops came to a halt; they no longer pursued
> Israel, nor did they fight anymore. (2 Samuel
> 2:28; emphasis mine)

David only lost 20 men compared to the 360 Benjamites that were killed. I bet both sides were grateful to hear that trumpet. Can you blow a trumpet today, announcing that you will fight over this matter no more? Put an end to whatever fight you are having and let the music bring a soothing end to the battle.

January 22

> Then I will ever *sing* in praise of your name
> and fulfill my vows day after day. (Psalm 61:8;
> emphasis mine)

Okay, sing, "God is so good, God is so good, God is so good, He's so good to me." Remember that song? That was on my mind this morning as I was thanking God in prayer. Our heavenly Father loves music and loves to be praised in song!

January 23

> The third angel sounded his *trumpet*, and
> a great star, blazing like a torch, fell from the
> sky on a third of the rivers and on the springs of
> water. (Revelation 8:10; emphasis mine)

In heaven, if you get to play a trumpet, you are really special. There are seven angels with seven trumpets, and every time a trumpet sounds, something incredible happens. Of course, that is true here on earth as well. People who play trumpet are really special to the Lord, and He loves to be glorified in the music.

January 24

> As well as some priests with *trumpets*,
> and also Zechariah son of Jonathan, the son
> of Shemaiah, the son of Mattaniah, the son of
> Micaiah, the son of Zakkur, the son of Asaph.
> (Nehemiah 12:35; emphasis mine)

Just as God has created every tribe, every language, and every nation, He has also blessed those He has chosen with the gift of being able to play music. If God blessed you with musical ability, play with all your heart as though playing for Him (Colossians 3:23).

January 25

> And he had provided him with a large room formerly used to store the grain offerings and incense and temple articles, and also the tithes of grain, new wine and olive oil prescribed for the Levites, *musicians* and gatekeepers, as well as the contributions for the priests. (Nehemiah 13:5; emphasis mine)

As a musician, you can take comfort in knowing that you have been identified and classified by God as someone He will provide for. He not only will provide for your needs but will make sure there is a place for you to go to get those provisions.

January 26

> Then I will go to the altar of God, to God, my joy and my delight. I will praise you with the *lyre*, O God, my God. (Psalm 43:4; emphasis mine)

Is playing music for God a sacrifice? Yes! There are many other things the world would love to have you do with your time instead of using your gifts and talents to praise God through music. The altar was a place for sacrifice. Playing music with all your heart can symbolize putting God first, willingly giving up anything and everything else to bring glory to Him.

January 27

> [*Jerusalem Under Siege*] Flee for safety, people of Benjamin! Flee from Jerusalem! Sound the *trumpet* in Tekoa! Raise the signal over Beth Hakkerem! For disaster looms out of the north, even terrible destruction. (Jeremiah 6:1; emphasis mine)

Trumpets have such a unique position in Scripture. Whenever something really significant is going to happen, a trumpet sounds.

Personally, I can't wait for the trumpet call of God when Jesus comes back. Hope it's today!

January 28

> [*An Army of Locusts*] Blow the *trumpet* in Zion; sound the alarm on my holy hill. Let all who live in the land tremble, for the day of the lord is coming. It is close at hand. (Joel 2:1; emphasis mine)

Someday, the sound of a trumpet will fill the air. It will not be for the siege of Jerusalem or the army of locusts about to invade but for the coming of the Lord. If today was the day, what would you do different? What plans would you change?

January 29

> I will clothe her priests with salvation, and her faithful people will ever *sing* for joy. (Psalm 132:16; emphasis mine)

Jesus said that He has given us His joy in order that our joy may be complete (John 15). Is your joy complete today? Let it overflow out of your heart in song. Sing!

January 30

> As I watched, I heard an eagle that was flying in midair call out in a loud voice, "Woe! Woe! Woe to the inhabitants of the earth, because of the *trumpet* blasts about to be sounded by the other three angels!" (Revelation 8:13; emphasis mine)

Such a significant instrument used by God. The sounds that can be made by the trumpet include many of God's emotions, sometimes soothing and calm, other times sharp blasts of warning.

January 31

> Praise him with the clash of *cymbals*, praise him with resounding *cymbals*. (Psalm 150:5; emphasis mine)

This has to be an anchor verse for every drummer in the world who praises God by playing the drums. I love how drummers integrate cymbals into the music, especially the bell of the cymbal. Praise God today for the percussionists and drummers that you know.

February 1

> Then Moses and the Israelites sang this
> song to the lord: "I will *sing* to the lord, for he
> is highly exalted. Both horse and driver he has
> hurled into the sea." (Exodus 15:1; emphasis
> mine)

The Lord allowed the Egyptians to follow the Israelites on dry ground, between two walls of water, only to destroy them. God may allow your persecutors to get close, but He is in control. That is something to sing about!

February 2

> Like one who takes away a garment on a
> cold day, or like vinegar poured on a wound, is
> one who *sings* songs to a heavy heart. (Proverbs
> 25:20; emphasis mine)

Sometimes, the best approach is to just be there for someone—not to rejoice, not to examine, not to advise, and not to sing, just to listen. Then after you complete your assignment, praise and sing to God, thanking Him for the opportunity to bring glory to Him.

February 3

> For the director of *music*. A psalm of
> David. May the lord answer you when you are
> in distress; may the name of the God of Jacob
> protect you. (Psalm 20:1; emphasis mine)

"I will call upon the Lord, He who is worthy to be praised. So shall I be saved from my enemies, I will call upon the Lord." Great song by Michael O'Shields.

February 4

> I will be fully satisfied as with the richest
> of aloes and cassia; from palaces adorned with
> ivory the *music* of the strings makes you glad.
> (Psalm 45:8; emphasis mine)

What a great expression of feelings! Being so satisfied with our relationship with the Lord is like having one of those fantastic feasts of your favorite foods (like lobster!). Loving the Lord with all our heart, all our soul, all our mind, and all our strength (Mark 12:30).

February 5

> The rest of the people—priests, Levites,
> gatekeepers, *musicians*, temple servants and all
> who separated themselves from the neighboring
> peoples for the sake of the Law of God, together
> with their wives and all their sons and daughters
> who are able to understand. (Nehemiah 10:28;
> emphasis mine)

As a musician, you have a special place in your heavenly Father's heart. You are separate from others, blessed with a gift He chose for you to bring glory to Him! No matter what instrument you play or your skill level, the music is symphonic to the Father's ears. What parent does not love to hear their kids play an instrument?

February 6

> All your robes are fragrant with myrrh and
> foods; with *singing* lips my mouth will praise
> you. (Psalm 63:5; emphasis mine)

Stringed instruments are amazing creations from God, enhanced by different shapes, woods, and a variety of strings, all for the purpose of creating sound. Jubal must have been delighted with his first stringed instrument.

February 7

> Away with the noise of your songs! I will
> not listen to the *music* of your harps. (Amos
> 5:23; emphasis mine)

Music is not a replacement or an alternative to obedience. God is a jealous God. He wants all of us all the time. If we walk down the broad road of life most of the week and then want to worship the Lord on Sunday by playing music, He says He will not listen.

February 8

> They *sing* to the music of timbrel and lyre;
> they make merry to the sound of the pipe. (Job
> 21:12; emphasis mine)

How incredible are the instruments that God has created! So many sounds, so many varieties! All for the purpose of worshipping Him. When we blend and harmonize with each other, I believe it brings special joy to our heavenly Father.

February 9

> For the director of *music*. To the tune of
> "Do Not Destroy." A psalm of Asaph. A song.
> We praise you, God, we praise you, for
> your Name is near; people tell of your wonderful
> deeds. (Psalm 75:1; emphasis mine)

I am not sure what the tune or melody of "Do Not Destroy" was, but what words we sing in worship are important. God also wants us to never forget what He has done for us. Can we write more songs that reflect on the journey He has us on?

February 10

> The Temple Musicians
> These are the men David put in charge of
> the *music* in the house of the lord after the ark

came to rest there. (1 Chronicles 6:31; emphasis mine)

Especially worship leaders! Blessed with the ability to choose songs, assign lead roles, arrange the delivery of the music set to augment the message that the Lord has prepared for the pastor or spokesperson. Musicians that play on praise teams are so gifted! They play with all their hearts as though playing for the Lord, not for men (Colossians 3:23).

February 11

[*The Musicians*] David, together with the commanders of the army, set apart some of the sons of Asaph, Heman and Jeduthun for the ministry of prophesying, accompanied by *harps*, lyres and cymbals. (1 Chronicles 25:1; emphasis mine)

What a great verse! I wonder what rehearsal for that would have been like! Attention, praise team. Today we need the guitarists, drummers, and harpists to accompany men who are prophesying. God is going to speak through these men, and He wants music in the background!

February 12

As for me, I will declare this forever; I will *sing* praise to the God of Jacob. (Psalm 75:9; emphasis mine)

The truth! As children of our heavenly Father, we can proclaim that there, in fact, will be a judgment day for those who have not accepted Jesus as personal Lord and Savior, and that He will deal with the wicked of the earth. The fact that we are exempt from judgment is certainly worth singing about!

February 13

> The joyful tambourines are stilled, the
> noise of the revelers has stopped, and the joyful
> *harp* is silent. (Isaiah 24:8; emphasis mine)

Can you imagine? When the Lord finally says, "Enough!" the devastation of the earth will be God's final victory over the forces of evil, and the music will stop! In chapter 25, we read about the praises that we will proclaim. Then chapter 26 is the song we will sing on that day!

February 14

> To gather the assembly, blow the *trumpets*,
> but not with the signal for setting out. (Numbers
> 10:7; emphasis mine)

The silver trumpets were used as signals to direct people, sometimes for assembly, sometimes for marching, sometimes for battle, and sometimes for festivals. As Paul wrote in his first letter to the church in Corinth, "We will all be changed—in a flash, in the twinkling of an eye, at the last trumpet." I bet it is a silver trumpet!

February 15

> *Sing* to him, *sing* praise to him; tell of all
> his wonderful acts. (1 Chronicles 16:9; emphasis
> mine)

Please share with someone today something that you know the Lord has done. Maybe share a story from Scripture or a personal event in your life. Your heavenly Father loves to hear you sing! Praise Him for what He has done, is doing, and will do!

February 16

> And those the lord has rescued will return.
> They will enter Zion with *singing*; everlasting
> joy will crown their heads. Gladness and joy will

overtake them, and sorrow and sighing will flee away. (Isaiah 35:10; emphasis mine)

Christians will have a joy that is so strong, it will permeate our souls. We have been ransomed, our sin debt paid in full by Jesus, and the sorrow and sighing will be done! Hallelujah!

February 17

Praise the lord, for the lord is good; *sing* praise to his name, for that is pleasant. (Psalm 135:3; emphasis mine)

There is something so special about singing a praise to our heavenly Father. Speaking praise is great as well, but to sing praise adds another dimension to the words.

February 18

Indeed, to them you are nothing more than one who *sings* love songs with a beautiful voice and plays an instrument well, for they hear your words but do not put them into practice. (Ezekiel 33:32; emphasis mine)

As the Lord spoke to Ezekiel, please know that sometimes your ability to play music and sing will be heard but not accepted. Music will open places in the heart for some, touching them in ways that words alone cannot. For others, they may even enjoy the music, the instruments, and the vocals, but there is no penetration in their hard hearts for what the Lord is saying through the music.

February 19

For the director of *music*. Of David. A psalm.
My God, whom I praise, do not remain silent. (Psalm 109:1; emphasis mine)

Interesting words to sing! How special is music to the ears of our heavenly Father? Even our prayer requests can be lifted up in song! David is being persecuted, and his prayer request asks God for delivery from these false accusers. Has anyone spoken lies about you? Has anyone repaid your goodness with evil? As you pray, sing out your request! See all of Psalm 109. There are twelve distinct requests by David for God to deal with these people who are treating David poorly.

February 20

> She looked, and there was the king, standing by his pillar at the entrance. The officers and the trumpeters were beside the king, and all the people of the land were rejoicing and blowing trumpets, and *musicians* with their instruments were leading the praises. Then Athaliah tore her robes and shouted, "Treason! Treason!" (2 Chronicles 23:13; emphasis mine)

The power of music! Leading worship on a day when a new king is crowned and Athaliah's plan to destroy the royal family is finished. Jehoiada showed his strength, and the coup was successful. She was taken out and killed. The celebration was led by musicians.

February 21

> The seventh time around, when the priests sounded the *trumpet* blast, Joshua commanded the army, "Shout! For the lord has given you the city!" (Joshua 6:16; emphasis mine)

Can you imagine being a trumpet player on that day? The stories that you could pass on to your children, generation after generation. A one-note concert that caused a one-word song, a shout that God used to collapse the walls of Jericho. Great story in Joshua 6.

February 22

> That my heart may *sing* your praises and not be silent. lord my God, I will praise you forever. (Psalm 30:12; emphasis mine)

Praying that in the middle of your today, you can remember all the good things God has done for you, that the rejoicing inside of you cannot be kept silent. As a child of God, we can rejoice in who our heavenly Father is.

February 23

> While he and all Israel were bringing up the ark of the lord with shouts and the sound of *trumpets*. (2 Samuel 6:15; emphasis mine)

On the journey from the house of Abinadab, David and thirty thousand men are bringing the ark back to Jerusalem. The whole house of Israel is celebrating with harps, lyres, tambourines, sistrums, and cymbals. Then when they reach Jerusalem, the trumpets are heard.

February 24

> Shebaniah, Joshaphat, Nethanel, Amasai, Zechariah, Benaiah and Eliezer the priests were to blow *trumpets* before the ark of God. (1 Chronicles 15:24; emphasis mine)

The unmistakable sound of the trumpet! Praising God for all you musicians that play any type of horn, for yours is a special talent you have been blessed with by God. Every instrument has a place in the great Christian orchestra. Imagine what the music in heaven will sound like!

February 25

> I also learned that the portions assigned to the Levites had not been given to them, and that all the Levites and *musicians* responsible for the service had gone back to their own fields. (Nehemiah 13:10; emphasis mine)

Nehemiah, led by God, puts reforms in place. He restores the Levites and musicians to their service positions. He was determined to make sure that the house of God was not neglected. Make sure that the musicians in your life are not neglected! Their talent is from God and is to be used for God's glory.

February 26

> For the director of *music*. To the tune of "Do Not Destroy." Of David. A miktam. When Saul had sent men to watch David's house in order to kill him.
> Deliver me from my enemies, O God; be my fortress against those who are attacking me. (Psalm 59:1; emphasis mine)

What was the tune of "Do Not Destroy"? What were the notes to the melody line of that song? The message was important enough to put the words to music that was familiar. Ever have a tune get stuck in your head for the day? Music is powerful!

February 27

> As well as the priests—Eliakim, Maaseiah, Miniamin, Micaiah, Elioenai, Zechariah and Hananiah with their *trumpets*. (Nehemiah 12:41; emphasis mine)

In verse 40, the two choirs that gave thanks took their places in the house of God, then the priests with their trumpets, and verse 43 tells us that "the sound of rejoicing in Jerusalem could be heard far away!" Can you sing and play music today with all your heart, all your soul, all your mind, and all your strength? Let it be heard far away!

February 28

> Make music to the lord with the harp, with the harp and the sound of *singing*. (Psalm 98:5; emphasis mine)

Oh, the sound of a single note, then two notes, then several notes combined to create a chord played on stringed instruments. Then add the voice that God has blessed you with and make music! Worship includes music from you! Either a song that you have heard or a new one that God is placing in your heart.

March 1

> The voice of the *singers* at the watering
> places. They recite the victories of the lord, the
> victories of his villagers in Israel. "Then the
> people of the lord went down to the city gates."
> (Judges 5:11; emphasis mine)

Mission: head to the city gates. Prerequisite: sing! What a great way to start our day before we enter the office, workplace, or wherever we are headed. Sing some praises to the Lord! Quote some Scripture verses back to Him. Praise Him for what He has done in your life!

March 2

> I amassed silver and gold for myself, and
> the treasure of kings and provinces. I acquired
> male and female *singers*, and a harem as well—
> the delights of a man's heart. (Ecclesiastes 2:8;
> emphasis mine)

Even among all the treasures of the world, all the available options to indulge oneself, singers are mentioned. God bless you that lift your voices to the King! Treasure the gift of music above all else. Play music for the Lord! Bring glory to Him today!

March 3

> For the director of *music*. A psalm of
> David. The king rejoices in your strength, lord.
> How great is his joy in the victories you give!
> (Psalm 21:1; emphasis mine)

The satisfaction of the win! The victory! The completion! All because the Lord enabled you to do it. What a great foundation to sing about! His strength in us. His power in us. Praise songs that bring glory to God for what He has done. Songs such as "Days of Elijah," Battle Hymn of the Republic," and "When the Roll Is Called Up Yonder" are timeless.

March 4

> Because you are my help, I *sing* in the shadow of your wings. (Psalm 63:7; emphasis mine)

Because He is our protector, our shepherd, our savior, and our all in all, we sing glory to Him. Praise God for all the music written to help us express our love to Jesus. "I love you Lord, and I lift my voice, to worship you oh my soul, rejoice, take joy my King, in what you hear, may it be a sweet, sweet sound in your ear."

March 5

> The people of Israel, including the Levites, are to bring their contributions of grain, new wine and olive oil to the storerooms, where the articles for the sanctuary and for the ministering priests, the gatekeepers and the *musicians* are also kept. "We will not neglect the house of our God." (Nehemiah 10:39; emphasis mine)

The "articles" for the musicians were kept in special rooms. Where do you keep your instrument? Other than a piano, it is probably kept in some type of protective case. The purpose, of course, is to protect the instrument that God has blessed you with the ability to play. The Holy Spirit provides protection for our souls, so they we may not be damaged. Praise God for protection!

March 6

> For the director of *music*. Of the Sons of Korah. According to alamoth. A song. God is our refuge and strength, an ever-present help in trouble. (Psalm 46:1; emphasis mine)

Alamoth is a musical term that denotes that this psalm was to be sung by soprano or female voices. The term is used on here and in 1 Chronicles 15:20. Praise God today for those women who can sing at that level, bringing the musical piece to an incredible level.

March 7

> You strum away on your harps like David
> and improvise on *musical* instruments. (Amos
> 6:5; emphasis mine)

Sounds like a jam session! The opportunity to create and perform without preparation can be exhilarating. Using a familiar structure such as a twelve-bar blues pattern is something most musicians can adapt to, regardless of what key the music is in. Praise God for the gifts and talents that He has given to musicians!

March 8

> But let all who take refuge in you be glad;
> let them ever *sing* for joy. Spread your protection
> over them, that those who love your name may
> rejoice in you. (Psalm 5:11; emphasis mine)

Let no one take away your joy! Even through trials and tribulations will most assuredly come into your life, take that deep breath and sing to God! Sing for joy in acknowledgment that He has you in His hands and that nothing that happens to you has not passed through His hands first. Sing for joy!

March 9

> As for Jeduthun, from his sons: Gedaliah,
> Zeri, Jeshaiah, Shimei, Hashabiah and
> Mattithiah, six in all, under the supervision of
> their father Jeduthun, who prophesied, using
> the *harp* in thanking and praising the lord. (1
> Chronicles 25:3; emphasis mine)

All these men were under the supervision of their father for the music of the temple of the Lord, with cymbals, lyres, and harps, for the ministry at the house of God. Praise God today if you were under the influence of an earthly father who encouraged you in music. Our heavenly Father also encourages you every day. Praise Him for that.

March 10

> They ministered with *music* before the tabernacle, the tent of meeting, until Solomon built the temple of the lord in Jerusalem. They performed their duties according to the regulations laid down for them. (1 Chronicles 6:32; emphasis mine)

These musicians and vocalists probably knew in advance what the worship set would be for that day and most likely would have their parts memorized. Just as when we memorize scripture, it grows in our hearts, the gift of music will bear fruit. Praise God today for your favorite pieces of music.

March 11

> Even in the case of lifeless things that make sounds, such as the pipe or *harp*, how will anyone know what tune is being played unless there is a distinction in the notes? (1 Corinthians 14:7; emphasis mine)

No instrument by itself can glorify God. It can be visible, it can be shiny and polished, and it can be inspiring to look at, but God has blessed individuals with the ability to play these instruments to bring glory to Him! Praise God for His creativity, for a musical scale that is standard for every instrument!

March 12

> *Sing* for joy to God our strength, shout aloud to the God of Jacob! (Psalm 81:1; emphasis mine)

Praise God for those moments when our emotion is so full of love and appreciation for what He has provided that we want to sing and shout! Sing for joy at those moments when your heart is so full of thanksgiving that you cannot keep quiet. Sing to God today!

March 13

> The sons of Aaron, the priests, are to blow the *trumpets*. This is to be a lasting ordinance for you and the generations to come. (Numbers 10:8; emphasis mine)

Praise God for the musicians that play the trumpet, one of God's favorite instruments. I am grateful for the many trumpet play- ers of our time. Praise God for the trumpet players that you know. Tell them how much you appreciate the gift that God has blessed them with. Pray for patience and earplugs for those who are listening to the new students !

March 14

> When the *trumpets* sounded, the army shouted, and at the sound of the *trumpet*, when the men gave a loud shout, the wall collapsed; so, everyone charged straight in, and they took the city. (Joshua 6:20; emphasis mine)

Even today, the trumpets are used to signify the start of something significant—the start of the Kentucky Derby, taps at a memorial, the announcement of someone special. God used the sound of trumpets to initiate one of the most spectacular victories in all of Scripture. After the sound of the trumpet, the voices shouted, and the walls collapsed in on their enemy. Praise God for His power!

March 15

> Rejoice in the lord and be glad, you are righteous; *sing*, all you who are upright in heart! (Psalm 32:11; emphasis mine)

Praise God for the fullness of having our hearts and minds set on Him. Through the Holy Spirit, our spirit connects in the most incredible ways. He fills us, He inspires us, and He loves us unconditionally. How can we not rejoice in Him? Sing something special to the Lord today. Praise God for music!

March 16

> For the grave cannot praise you, death cannot *sing* your praise; those who go down to the pit cannot hope for your faithfulness. (Isaiah 38:18; emphasis mine)

Hezekiah had wept and prayed to the Lord. Hearing his prayers and knowing his tears, the Lord blessed Hezekiah with fifteen additional years of life. Hezekiah so worshipped the Lord that he lamented on the fact that he could not praise the Lord if he were in the grave. Praise God that you know where you will be praising God for eternity—in heaven!

March 17

> I will turn your religious festivals into mourning and all your *singing* into weeping. I will make all of you wear sackcloth and shave your heads. I will make that time like mourning for an only son and the end of it like a bitter day. (Amos 8:10; emphasis mine)

Wow! Is it possible that through these events that the Israelites loved so much that they forgot to bring glory to the Lord? God is a jealous God, and we should never place anything or anyone in a higher position than He deserves. That even includes music! In this case, the consequence for their sin seems somewhat extreme. God's love for us is also extreme as He let His one and only Son die on the cross to pay for our sin debt.

March 18

> For the director of *music*. With stringed instruments. A psalm of Asaph. A song. God is renowned in Judah; in Israel his name is great. (Psalm 76:1; emphasis mine)

Having a theme for the music that you are writing makes the creating a little easier. Here the them$e for this psalm is that God is renowned in Judah and His name is great in Israel. God was celebrated, famous, esteemed, distinguished, and loved with stringed instruments, which add depth to the music. Praise God today for all the musicians that play stringed instruments!

March 19

> Then Absalom sent secret messengers throughout the tribes of Israel to say, "As soon as you hear the sound of the *trumpets*, then say, 'Absalom is king in Hebron.'" (2 Samuel 15:10; emphasis mine)

The significance of the sound of the trumpet! Everyone knew that the sound of the trumpet meant something was about to happen, something to be done. What does God use to get your attention? Praise God today for all the ways He uses to get our attention and thank Him for the trumpet players!

March 20

> Now write down this song and teach it to the Israelites and have them *sing* it, so that it may be a witness for me against them. (Deuteronomy 31:19; emphasis mine)

Ugh! Not only was the music director to write down the words to a song authored by God, he had to teach the Israelites to sing a song that provides testimony that the Lord will use against them. Ugh!

March 21

> The whole assembly bowed in worship, while the *musicians* played, and the trumpets sounded. All this continued until the sacrifice of the burnt offering was completed. (2 Chronicles 29:28; emphasis mine)

Participating in a worship service where we are led to bow on one (or both) knee adds something special to the moment. The act of submission to God's authority, to His rule, accepting His lordship over our lives is pleasing to Him. Music fills such places in our hearts like nothing else can. The praise team leads, and we follow. Praise God for our worship leaders and members of the praise teams.

March 22

> Let the rivers clap their hands, let the mountains *sing* together for joy. (Psalm 98:8; emphasis mine)

What a fantastic visual of how everything that God has created worships Him—the rivers clapping as the waves crash into the shores, the mountains full of trees and the wildlife singing in response to God's call. Today, clap your hands and sing out to your heavenly Father, thanking Him for His creation and music!

March 23

> The fourth angel sounded his *trumpet*, and a third of the sun was struck, a third of the moon, and a third of the stars, so that a third of them turned dark. A third of the day was without light, and also a third of the night. (Revelation 8:12; emphasis mine)

When the end-times come, God's wrath will be devastating and complete. In His mercy, there will still be opportunities for people to come to Christ during this period of tribulation. The significance of one of God's favorite instruments, the trumpet, is still in use. Pray for those who have not yet accepted Jesus as personal Lord and Savior.

March 24

> In frenzied excitement it eats up the ground; it cannot stand still when the *trumpet* sounds. (Job 39:24; emphasis mine)

The Clydesdale and the Belgian horse breeds are two of the largest in the horse family. God created these magnificent animals and wired them for their assignments. Even the horse knows what it was created for and is anxious to perform. Are you ready to perform for God? Are you ready to use the gifts and talents He has blessed you with? Praise Him for your next assignment!

March 25

> For the director of *music*. With stringed instruments. A psalm of David. Answer me when I call to you, my righteous God. Give me relief from my distress; have mercy on me and hear my prayer. (Psalm 4:1; emphasis mine)

Music written for stringed instruments with a depth of feeling, as this is a request for God to answer. Praise God for all the types of stringed instruments and the depth that sound adds to our prayer request.

Praise God for all the stringed instrument players in your life!

March 26

> I appointed watchmen over you and said, "Listen to the sound of the *trumpet*!" But you said, "We will not listen." (Jeremiah 6:17; emphasis mine)

God has a hierarchy for everything. When He places someone in authority over you or places you in authority over someone else, He expects obedience. When God sounds the trumpet in your life, or whatever He uses to get you attention, obey what He has called you to do. Praise Him!

March 27

> For the director of *music*. Of David. A psalm. You have searched me, lord, and you know me. (Psalm 139:1; emphasis mine)

Rejoice! The creator of heaven and earth also created you, knit you in the womb. He knows everything about you, specifically the gifts and talents He has blessed you with. The song "Knowing You" is a wonderful worship song, stirring the heart to draw close to Him. Sing to God today!

March 28

> Blow the *trumpet* in Zion, declare a holy fast, call a sacred assembly. (Joel 2:15; emphasis mine)

I love that God uses a musical instrument to initiate an event. The distinguished sound of the trumpet was something everyone was familiar with, and they knew the fact that they would be required to do something, to participate in an event. Praise God for every event that God has orchestrated for you!

March 29

> For there our captors asked us for songs, our tormentors demanded songs of joy; they said, "*Sing* us one of the songs of Zion!" (Psalm 137:3; emphasis mine)

Music is such a powerful voice of God! Even those who are enemies of us can appreciate the power of music. Playing joyful music when we are in a time of stress requires much prayer. When we turn our attention to the opportunity before us and not on ourselves, God will bless our efforts! Sing today!

March 30

> For the director of *music*. To the tune of "The Lily of the Covenant." A miktam of David. For teaching. When he fought Aram Naharaim and Aram Zobah, and when Joab returned and struck down twelve thousand Edomites in the Valley of Salt. You have rejected us, God, and

burst upon us; you have been angry—now restore us! (Psalm 60:1; emphasis mine)

Miktam is a unique word used only six times, all in Psalms, and only by David. The common accepted meaning is "an epigram," which is a pithy saying or remark expressing an idea in a clever and amusing way. Therefore, the song was to be joyful. Rejoice when you are restored, when your spirit is renewed in fellowship with the Father.

March 31

On the Lord's Day I was in the Spirit, and I heard behind me a loud voice like a *trumpet*. (Revelation 1:10; emphasis mine)

What a wonderful feeling it is to be in tune with the Holy Spirit. When He touches us in that special way, He encourages us and stands in the gap for us. The voice of Jesus, like the sound of a trumpet, penetrated John's soul. Praise God that He can penetrate our souls with music, with song, and with Scripture.

April 1

> *Sing* to the lord, all the earth; proclaim
> his salvation day after day. (1 Chronicles 16:23;
> emphasis mine)

Especially on this day, marked as April Fools'. The Lord mentions fools and the activities of fools and the consequences of foolish behavior in Scripture. This is good advice for today and every day. Sing to the Lord! Sing with all your heart, all your soul, and all your strength!

April 2

> Flowers appear on the earth; the season of
> *singing* has come; the cooing of doves is heard in
> our land. (Song of Songs 2:12; emphasis mine)

Is it not simply amazing that God, at His appointed time, awakens the flowers and trees and everything that He put to sleep over the winter in an incredible display of majesty and power? No wonder it is a time for singing!

April 3

> For the director of *music*. To the tune of
> "The Doe of the Morning." A psalm of David.
> My God, my God, why have you forsaken me?
> Why are you so far from saving me, so far from
> my cries of anguish? (Psalm 22:1; emphasis
> mine)

As far as I know, there is no sheet music for "The Doe of the Morning." I wonder how robust the instrumentation of that tune would be, how dramatic the bridge would sound. This verse is quoted by Jesus while on the cross, the one moment in time that He wanted the Father to take away. It was not dying on the cross to pay for our sin, His love compelled Him to do that. But for a moment, He had to feel the separation from the Father that sin causes.

April 4

> The meadows are covered with flocks and
> the valleys are mantled with grain; they shout
> for joy and *sing*. (Psalm 65:13; emphasis mine)

Everything that God has created worships Him—everything. From the animals to the crops, from the trees to the seas. We should do no less. Shout! Sing! Bring glory to the one who created you.

April 5

> The chief officer of the Levites in Jerusalem
> was Uzzi son of Bani, the son of Hashabiah, the
> son of Mattaniah, the son of Mika. Uzzi was one
> of Asaph's descendants, who were the *musicians*
> responsible for the service of the house of God.
> (Nehemiah 11:22; emphasis mine)

Praise God for all of you that serve on a praise team or bring music to any assembly where God is glorified. That could be the church, a nursing home, or a prison. It is an awesome responsibility, one that fills your soul like nothing else.

April 6

> For the director of *music*. Of the Sons
> of Korah. A psalm. Clap your hands, all you
> nations, shout to God with cries of joy. (Psalm
> 47:1; emphasis mine)

There is a term called *hand praise*, and that allows for those who are not playing an instrument to participate in the worship music. Clap your hands and cry out to God with joy. Never be ashamed to lift your hands in worship, to clap your hands in time with the music, to sing at the top of your lungs! When the music stops, praise God for the musicians that lifted their music up to God. Clap your hands!

April 7

> The Sovereign lord is my strength; he makes my feet like the feet of a deer; he enables me to tread on the heights. For the director of *music*. On my stringed instruments. (Habakkuk 3:19; emphasis mine)

You know how it is when you hear a song that you cannot sit still to. Your feet tap, your fingers play the drums, your body starts to move. The music is so powerful that it inspires you to move. This song was inspiring to hear. May you hear one today that strengthens you!

April 8

> The one who was dying blessed me; I made the widow's heart *sing*. (Job 29:13; emphasis mine)

There may be no more appropriate place for music than at a funeral. Every note and word seem to have enhanced meaning, something special in the feeling. Comforting a widow is special to the Lord, as He has called us to look after widows and orphans. Music helps!

April 9

> For the director of *music*. For Jeduthun. Of Asaph. A psalm. I cried out to God for help; I cried out to God to hear me. (Psalm 77:1; emphasis mine)

I wonder if this might have been one of the original blues formats. Blues music, many times, is heartfelt brokenness put into words and dramatic notes. It is a unique platform to cry out to God for help. May you find comfort in song today, even if it is a blues day.

April 10

> Here are the men who served, together with their sons: From the Kohathites: Heman,

the *musician*, the son of Joel, the son of Samuel. (1 Chronicles 6:33; emphasis mine)

All musicians are special to God. Here, Heman gets mentioned by name and, of course, his lineage. Your name is also written in a book that has not been read yet. As a musician, you have been blessed with a gift that is to be used to bring glory to God.

April 11

They entered Jerusalem and went to the temple of the lord with *harps* and lyres and trumpets. (2 Chronicles 20:28; emphasis mine)

There are two types of stringed instruments mentioned here along with the trumpets. Harp music might be the most heavenly sounding instrument next to a grand piano. Lyres are guitars in the early stages. The music would have been interesting to listen to, and certainly challenging to sing to, but the sound would be wonderful to God's ears.

April 12

As they make music they will *sing*, "All my fountains are in you." (Psalm 87:7; emphasis mine)

What great imagery comes to mind when you read those words? Jesus said that He would become a fountain of living water that would cause us to never thirst for Him. There is a contemporary song titled "There Is a Fountain" that says it is drawn from Emmanuel's veins. Indeed, all our fountains are in Him.

April 13

And when he had taken it, the four living creatures and the twenty-four elders fell down before the Lamb. Each one had a *harp*, and they were holding golden bowls full of incense, which are the prayers of God's people. (Revelation 5:8; emphasis mine)

What a great concert that would have been to go to—harp music, prayers of God's people being sung, incense and music in the air, worship in heaven! Hope you are excited about that day when we will hear, sing, and play music for the Lord in our new home.

April 14

> When you go into battle in your own land against an enemy who is oppressing you, sound a blast on the *trumpets*. Then you will be remembered by the lord your God and rescued from your enemies. (Numbers 10:9; emphasis mine)

God says to use that musical instrument to call Him, not just prayer, not just crying out, but blowing the sound that signifies something important to God not only in music but in events that are important. Praise God for our trumpet players.

April 15

> *Sing* joyfully to the lord, you righteous; it is fitting for the upright to praise him. (Psalm 33:1; emphasis mine)

Into the heart of the Psalms, the instruction is to sing! Praise the Lord with your voice! Let Him know that you love Him, need Him, adore Him, and depend on Him. Sing it out!

April 16

> The lord will save me, and we will *sing* with stringed instruments all the days of our lives in the temple of the lord. (Isaiah 38:20; emphasis mine)

When our confidence is in the Lord, knowing that He is not up there wringing His hands, wondering what to do about it, we can have joy in our praise. We can sing in the midst of any situation all the days of our lives!

April 17

> *Sing*, Daughter Zion; shout aloud, Israel!
> Be glad and rejoice with all your heart, Daughter
> Jerusalem! (Zephaniah 3:14; emphasis mine)

Jesus said, "Love the Lord with all your heart, and with all your soul, and with all your mind, and with all your strength." Someday we will be walking the streets of the New Jerusalem—with Him. Sing about that!

April 18

> For the director of *music*. A psalm of
> David. Rescue me, lord, from evildoers; protect
> me from the violent. (Psalm 140:1; emphasis
> mine)

When our relationship is right with God, we can experience the peace that passes understanding, even in the midst of the trial. Praise God for His protection.

April 19

> When he arrived there, he blew a *trumpet*
> in the hill country of Ephraim, and the Israelites
> went down with him from the hills, with him
> leading them. (Judges 3:27; emphasis mine)

Almost every time a significant event is about to happen in Scripture, God uses one of His favorite instruments, the trumpet. Praise God for the horn players that you know, especially the trumpet players.

April 20

> When the men were returning home after
> David had killed the Philistine, the women
> came out from all the towns of Israel to meet
> King Saul with *singing* and dancing, with joyful

songs and with timbrels and lyres. (1 Samuel 18:6; emphasis mine)

A concert of praise for God, celebrating a great victory over the Philistines. Singing, musical instruments, dancing, and people filled with joy over the victory. Let music help you face and defeat the giants in your life.

April 21

The workers labored faithfully. Over them to direct them were Jahath and Obadiah, Levites descended from Merari, and Zechariah and Meshullam, descended from Kohath. The Levites—all who were skilled in playing *musical* instruments. (2 Chronicles 34:12; emphasis mine)

Praise God for all the musicians in our life! How much better is our worship because of the instruments that God has created. His creativity never ceases to amaze us. Look at all the music He has inspired with only seven major keys!

April 22

Let them *sing* before the lord, for he comes to judge the earth. He will judge the world in righteousness and the peoples with equity. (Psalm 98:9; emphasis mine)

Jesus told His disciples just hours before being arrested that He will send the Holy Spirit, who will convict the world of guilt in regard to sin and righteousness and judgment. Jesus sent the Holy Spirit and told Him to take from what was His and make it known to us. Part of that assignment includes inspiration for music!

April 23

Then Joab sounded the *trumpet*, and the troops stopped pursuing Israel, for Joab halted them. (2 Samuel 18:16; emphasis mine)

It was possibly the loudest instrument available at that time and used for many applications—not stringed instruments, not drums but trumpets. You can find trumpet in Scripture 114 times. What a versatile instrument.

April 24

> And Benaiah and Jahaziel the priests were to blow the *trumpets* regularly before the ark of the covenant of God. (1 Chronicles 16:6; emphasis mine)

Among all the other assignments that priests would have, I bet Benaiah and Jahaziel loved getting to play their trumpets more than anything. Musicians love to use the gifts and talents that God has blessed them with. Even if you do not play the trumpet, use whatever gift God has blessed you with today!

April 25

> For the director of *music*. For pipes. A psalm of David. Listen to my words, lord, consider my lament. (Psalm 5:1; emphasis mine)

Jubal, mentioned in Genesis 4:21, is credited with being the father of all who play stringed instruments and pipes. Pipes would include early versions of flutes. Since the music is for a lament, the pipes would provide some soothing background for the passionate plea to God.

April 26

> For the director of *music*. With stringed instruments. Of David. Hear my cry, O God; listen to my prayer. (Psalm 61:1; emphasis mine)

A cry out to God in prayer with stringed instruments. Harp music comes to mind when I consider David, who was a musician himself, crying out to God regarding his circumstances. Stringed instruments, especially the harp, provide incredible background for prayer and meditation.

April 27

> At the blast of the *trumpet* it snorts, "Aha!"
> It catches the scent of battle from afar, the shout
> of commanders and the battle cry. (Job 39:25;
> emphasis mine)

In verses 19–25, God is asking Job if he understands the creation of the horse—the horse that is designed by God, including the instinct to respond to the sound of the trumpet. Certainly, one of God's favorite instruments!

April 28

> And if you say, "No, we will go and live
> in Egypt, where we will not see war or hear
> the *trumpet* or be hungry for bread." (Jeremiah
> 42:14; emphasis mine)

The sound of the trumpet was recognized, and action was required on the part of all who heard the sound. The remnant of Israelites were petitioning Jeremiah to plead their case before God, and in His response, the trumpet is also mentioned.

April 29

> How can we *sing* the songs of the lord
> while in a foreign land? (Psalm 137:4; emphasis
> mine)

Sometimes it is hard to imagine when or even if joy will return to us. On our own we cannot satisfy that empty place inside with anything meaningful. Only Jesus can fill that place. We can look to Him, sing to Him, and praise Him with all our heart! Regardless of where we find ourselves this side of heaven, we can rejoice and sing!

April 30

> So, all Israel brought up the ark of the
> covenant of the lord with shouts, with the
> sounding of rams' horns and trumpets, and of

cymbals, and the playing of *lyres* and harps. (1 Chronicles 15:28; emphasis mine)

Ever want to just start over? To begin again, to be renewed, and to know that our God is a God of second chances. In this story, the ark is being returned, and all of Israel is rejoicing, with an emphasis on music and singing praise to the Lord. Let today be a day of restarting and renewal!

May 1

> Kenaniah the head Levite was in charge of the *singing*; that was his responsibility because he was skillful at it. (1 Chronicles 15:22; emphasis mine)

Worship leaders are truly gifted people. The praise team is blessed, the congregation is blessed, and God is pleased because of the time and effort that worship leaders put into their assignments. Take a minute today to thank your worship leader and praise God for the gift!

May 2

> [The Song of the Vineyard] I will *sing* for the one I love a song about his vineyard: My loved one had a vineyard on a fertile hillside. (Isaiah 5:1; emphasis mine)

The power of music! A song touches our heart and creates feelings inside that are almost indescribable at times. Emotion drawn from deep within, initiated by music, articulated in song. Sing today to one you love!

May 3

> For the director of music. A psalm of David. In you, lord, I have taken refuge; let me never be put to shame; deliver me in your righteousness. (Psalm 31:1; emphasis mine)

Songs of deliverance! Like "Days of Elijah" and "Awesome God!" Great songs of being renewed, like "Amazing Grace." Thank You, Lord, for the hymns that You have inspired over the centuries, in all seasons.

May 4

> *Sing* the glory of his name; make his praise
> glorious. (Psalm 66:2; emphasis mine)

Think of the song "How Great Thou Art." It is a worship song like no other. It honors our Lord's creation, the love that it took to sacrifice His only Son so that we may have life in Him. Read the words to this hymn today and then sing it, play it, rejoice in it! It is a glorious praise song!

May 5

> The *musicians* were under the king's orders,
> which regulated their daily activity. (Nehemiah
> 11:23; emphasis mine)

Just like sheet music provides structure for the piece being played, the king ordered the activities of the musicians. It was an honor to play for the king. It will be an honor to play for our King someday!

May 6

> For the director of *music*. Of the Sons of
> Korah. According to alamoth. A song. God is
> our refuge and strength, an ever-present help in
> trouble. (Psalm 46:1; emphasis mine)

God says, "I am your refuge; your place of safety; your place of protection. I am your strength; your source of endurance; your shepherd." The depth of meaning to the love that God has for us is certainly worth singing about!

May 7

> You strum away on your harps like David
> and improvise on *musical* instruments. (Amos
> 6:5; emphasis mine)

This verse is part of a warning that Amos is bringing to the nation of Israel. God is terribly upset with their neglect and how prideful they have become. Even mentioning the music from harps and other instruments clearly shows that music that does not honor Him or that is not played in the proper time is offensive to God. We have to remember as musicians that when we play is as important as when we play.

May 8

> But let all who take refuge in you be glad;
> let them ever *sing* for joy. Spread your protection
> over them, that those who love your name may
> rejoice in you. (Psalm 5:11; emphasis mine)

John's gospel letter states that even though some did not recognize Jesus when He came, others that did accept Him are given the right to become children of God! As a child of God, sing to your heavenly Father! Rejoice in His goodness.

May 9

> As for Jeduthun, from his sons: Gedaliah,
> Zeri, Jeshaiah, Shimei, Hashabiah and
> Mattithiah, six in all, under the supervision of
> their father Jeduthun, who prophesied, using
> the *harp* in thanking and praising teh lord. (1
> Chronicles 25:3; emphasis mine)

A prophet and a worship leader! All six of his sons praising God. Was Jeduthun the only harp player? Did all six play harps? That would have been an incredible sound. Praise God today for any harp player that you know. The sound from a modern-day harp is as beautiful as any stringed instrument ever made.

May 10

> They ministered with *music* before the
> tabernacle, the tent of meeting, until Solomon
> built the temple of the lord in Jerusalem.
> They performed their duties according to the
> regulations laid down for them. (1 Chronicles
> 6:32; emphasis mine)

Ministering with music. What great opportunities we have as musicians to touch places in the heart like nothing else can. Music permeates the soul and connects with the Holy Spirit to bring glory to God in special ways. Consider how you might use your gifts and talents as musicians today.

May 11

> Even in the case of lifeless things that make sounds, such as the pipe or *harp*, how will anyone know what tune is being played unless there is a distinction in the notes? (1 Corinthians 14:7; emphasis mine)

Praise God for all the major keys! The tone of an A is the same no matter what instrument it is played on. The same for the other major keys and all the variations of those keys, with sharps and flats and combinations. Notes are distinctive!

May 12

> *Sing* for joy to God our strength, shout aloud to the God of Jacob! (Psalm 81:1; emphasis mine)

The command is to sing! Sing to God, your heavenly Father today. All of creation does! Sing to Him loudly and with confidence that regardless of how you think it sounds, when it reaches heaven, it is symphonic!

May 13

> The sons of Aaron, the priests, are to blow the *trumpets*. This is to be a lasting ordinance for you and the generations to come. (Numbers 10:8; emphasis mine)

Some instruments carry more weight than others. They have a distinction in their purpose. The use of trumpets is symbolic in Scripture, always identifying a significant event. Praise God today for the trumpet players that you may know personally.

May 14

> When the *trumpets* sounded, the army shouted, and at the sound of the *trumpet*, when the men gave a loud shout, the wall collapsed; so, everyone charged straight in, and they took the city. (Joshua 6:20; emphasis mine)

One of the greatest displays of God's power and majesty is the destruction of Jericho. The trumpets of ram's horns were blown for six straight days, making one trip around the city. On the seventh day, they marched around the city seven times, and then after one long blast, the men shouted, and the walls collapsed. Incredible.

May 15

> Rejoice in the lord and be glad, you righteous; *sing*, all you who are upright in heart! (Psalm 32:11; emphasis mine)

Scripture tells us that God looks at our hearts. What is our motivation? When we are right with God, we can sing! We can be glad! We can enter His gates with thanksgiving in our hearts. Rejoice in your salvation! God's provision for your new home!

May 16

> For the grave cannot praise you, death cannot *sing* your praise; those who go down to the pit cannot hope for your faithfulness. (Isaiah 38:18; emphasis mine)

Isaiah acknowledges what each person has wondered about after death. For those of us who are in Christ, we will sing praise forever. For those who have rejected His offer of salvation, there will be no praise and no hope.

May 17

> I will turn your religious festivals into mourning and all your *singing* into weeping. I

will make all of you wear sackcloth and shave
your heads. I will make that time like mourning
for an only son and the end of it like a bitter day.
(Amos 8:10; emphasis mine)

A further warning from the Lord through the prophet Amos. Could the United States be headed for a similar judgment? Israel had abandoned God's commands, ignored His instruction, and was not obedient. Pray that our hearts are right when we go about our day, especially when we sing!

May 18

For the director of *music*. With stringed
instruments. A psalm of Asaph. A song. God is
renowned in Judah; in Israel his name is great.
(Psalm 76:1; emphasis mine)

Love these praise songs! Love the sounds of stringed instruments! Praise God for you who play any type of stringed instrument, and please encourage someone you know today who plays an instrument—pianos, guitars, ukuleles, violins, harps, cellos, bass, and banjo!

May 19

Then Absalom sent secret messengers
throughout the tribes of Israel to say, "As soon
as you hear the sound of the *trumpets*, then say,
'Absalom is king in Hebron.'" (2 Samuel 15:10;
emphasis mine)

As always throughout Scripture, the trumpet is the one instrument that is used to signify something important. Absalom used a common practice for his own edification. Encourage each other as musicians to never use the gift that God gave us to bring glory to ourselves.

May 20

Now write down this song and teach it to
the Israelites and have them *sing* it, so that it may

be a witness for me against them. (Deuteronomy 31:19; emphasis mine)

What a bizarre assignment! The Lord has told Moses that he is about to die and that the nation of Israel will soon turn to other gods, so God already knows this and has Moses write the words to a song and teach it to the people before he is called to heaven. It does, however, manifest the importance of music to God.

May 21

The whole assembly bowed in worship, while the *musicians* played, and the trumpets sounded. All this continued until the sacrifice of the burnt offering was completed. (2 Chronicles 29:28; emphasis mine)

Think about this the next time you take communion: Jesus replaced the need to have animal sacrifices by shedding His own blood, but we still are able to praise God through music as part of our worship. The vision of a whole assembly bowing in worship is beautiful.

May 22

Let the rivers clap their hands, let the mountains *sing* together for joy. (Psalm 98:8; emphasis mine)

It is amazing that God has created a way for everything He has made to be able to worship Him. The rivers, the oceans and seas, the mountains, trees, and flowers—all have their own designed way to worship the Lord. Hear the birds singing worship this morning?

May 23

The fourth angel sounded his *trumpet,* and a third of the sun was struck, a third of the moon, and a third of the stars, so that a third of them turned dark. A third of the day was without light, and also a third of the night. (Revelation 8:12; emphasis mine)

Here is the most mentioned instrument in scripture, the trumpet. After it is sounded (note: after it is used for what it was intended), then action takes place. Let us use the instrument that God blessed us with the ability to play for His glory.

May 24

> In frenzied excitement it eats up the ground; it cannot stand still when the *trumpet* sounds. (Job 39:24; emphasis mine)

This is a reference to the impact that the sound of the trumpet has on the horse, one of God's most magnificent creatures, and He has the animal already wired to react to the sound of the trumpet. Praise God today for the trumpet players in your life.

May 25

> For the director of *music*. With stringed instruments. A psalm of David. Answer me when I call to you, my righteous God. Give me relief from my distress; have mercy on me and hear my prayer. (Psalm 4:1; emphasis mine)

What an inspiration prayer is for writing music. Think of the great songs that Holy Spirit has inspired, such as "Sweet Hour of Prayer," especially with stringed instruments that can provide such a soothing background and melody for prayerful worship. Praise God for those who write music that brings glory to Him.

May 26

> I appointed watchmen over you and said, "Listen to the sound of the *trumpet*!" But you said, "We will not listen." (Jeremiah 6:17; emphasis mine)

This is one of the numerous occasions in Scripture where the assignment calls for the sound of a trumpet. Do you have an assignment that calls for you to listen to the sound of an instrument? Pray for those that are learning to listen!

May 27

> For the director of *music*. Of David. A psalm. You have searched me, lord, and you know me. (Psalm 139:1; emphasis mine)

So many songs have been inspired by the Psalms. "Search Me O God," "Create in Me a Clean Heart" are a couple. The fact that our heavenly Father knows everything about us and cares about what we do and how we do it is almost too much to comprehend. Praise God that He does know us and loves us anyway!

May 28

> Blow the *trumpet* in Zion, declare a holy fast, call a sacred assembly. (Joel 2:15; emphasis mine)

Big announcements are initiated by the sound of one of the loudest instruments that God has created, the trumpet! The sound can be heard for great distances. Praise God today for all the notes that a trumpet can play and for those who skillfully play the horns.

May 29

> For there our captors asked us for songs, our tormentors demanded songs of joy; they said, "*Sing* us one of the songs of Zion!" (Psalm 137:3; emphasis mine)

It is ironic that the captors preferred to hear the live music of the Israelites than their own musicians. Music has the ability to bring joy, to instill a sense of happiness and fill an empty place inside of us that nothing else can. Praise God today for the impact that music has had on your life!

May 30

> For the director of *music*. To the tune of "The Lily of the Covenant." A miktam of David. For teaching. When he fought Aram Naharaim

and Aram Zobah, and when Joab returned and struck down twelve thousand Edomites in the Valley of Salt. You have rejected us, God, and burst upon us; you have been angry—now restore us! (Psalm 60:1; emphasis mine)

Don't you wonder what the tune of "The Lily of the Covenant" sounded like? The melody line had to have been familiar, so putting new words to a tune would be much easier to learn. Many of the Christian songs written in the early days of this country were written to already established tunes so that learning would be quicker. Music was again employed to reach out to God!

May 31

[*The Throne in Heaven*] After this I looked, and there before me was a door standing open in heaven. And the voice I had first heard speaking to me like a *trumpet* said, "Come up here, and I will show you what must take place after this." (Revelation 1:10; emphasis mine)

Oh my goodness! Here is the sound of the trumpet, not the trumpet itself, being used to speak to John. I bet the sound was majestic! Praise God for all the vocalists and all the ranges of their voices. From soprano to bass, the voices that God has blessed us with to bring glory to Him through worship.

Thank a vocalist for their voice today!

June 1

> After consulting the people, Jehoshaphat
> appointed men to *sing* to the lord and to praise
> him for the splendor of his holiness as they
> went out at the head of the army, saying: "Give
> thanks to the lord, for his love endures forever."
> (2 Chronicles 20:21; emphasis mine)

Jehoshaphat appointed men to sing! Notice where they are
located, out in front of the army! Attention, all vocalists: you are also
appointed to lead us in worship, giving thanks to the Lord. Every day
His love endures forever. Praise God today for the singers that you
know.

June 2

> *Sing* to the lord, for he has done glorious
> things; let this be known to all the world. (Isaiah
> 12:5; emphasis mine)

What a great way to start the day, to endure the day, and to end
the day—by singing to the Lord! Praise Him for the glory you see
every moment of every minute of every day: The flowers, the trees, the
sky, with shades of blue and all different types of clouds. For streams,
rivers, and seas. Even for grass and the aroma of a freshly mowed lawn.
Glorious!

June 3

> About midnight Paul and Silas were
> praying and *singing* hymns to God, and the
> other prisoners were listening to them. (Acts
> 16:25; emphasis mine)

Singing has an incredible effect on your soul and those who hear you. Regardless of the circumstances, you can sing even your requests to God. He hears and touches your soul with joy. Note the other encouragement here: memorize the hymns as they will be a comfort to you.

June 4

> You created the north and the south,
> Tabor and Hermon *sing* for joy at your name.
> (Psalm 89:12; emphasis mine)

An interesting perspective! It is God who created all directions, and even for that we can sing praises to Him! Praise God that we have a compass that gives us direction on the outside and a moral compass that guides us on the inside. Sing for joy!

June 5

> [*Dedication of the Wall of Jerusalem*] At the dedication of the wall of Jerusalem, the Levites were sought out from where they lived and were brought to Jerusalem to celebrate joyfully the dedication with songs of thanksgiving and with the *music* of cymbals, harps and lyres. (Nehemiah 12:27; emphasis mine)

What an interesting praise team! Cymbals, harps, and guitars. All providing the music for the singers and the concert of songs of thanksgiving and praise to God. Praise God today for the drummers that you know, the harp players, and all the guitarists! Praise God for the singers!

June 6

> Praise the lord with the harp; make *music*
> to him on the ten-stringed lyre. (Psalm 33:2;
> emphasis mine)

The closest guitar we have to the ten-stringed lyre is the twelvestring guitar, which has ten different strings, and two strings are duplicated. A very full sound! I think it is a wonderful complement to the harp. It is majestic to listen to the modern-day harpist. Praise God for harp players and twelve-string guitar players.

June 7

> I will give thanks to the lord because of his righteousness; I will *sing* the praises of the name of the lord Most High. (Psalm 9:2; emphasis mine)

"Lord I Lift Your Name on High" is a favorite of many Christians. Songs that praise the name of the Lord are special, as well as the songs that praise Him for all He has done. "Blessed Be the Name of the Lord" is another favorite in praise settings. Praise the Lord today!

June 8

> Every stroke the lord lays on them with his punishing club will be to the *music* of timbrels and harps, as he fights them in battle with the blows of his arm. (Isaiah 30:32; emphasis mine)

Timbrels are like tambourines and would make an interesting accompaniment to the harp. Notice the application of this music: it establishes the beat of the beating that the Lord is giving to the enemy. What a classic way to listen to music! Praise God for tambourine players!

June 9

> The *music* of harpists and *musicians*, pipers and trumpeters, will never be heard in you again. No worker of any trade will ever be found in you again. The sound of a millstone will never be heard in you again. (Revelation 18:22; emphasis mine)

There will come a time when a mighty angel of the Lord will destroy Babylon. The great city that has become the home base for evil and every kind of evil practice. There is a warning to all the remaining people. This is a time after the rapture. Praise God that you belong to Jesus Christ and will not suffer the consequences that Babylon will endure.

June 10

> David told the leaders of the Levites to appoint their fellow Levites as *musicians* to make a joyful sound with *musical* instruments: lyres, harps and cymbals. (1 Chronicles 15:16; emphasis mine)

Remember that David was a musician himself. He instructed the Levite musicians to make a joyful sound with their instruments. If you are a musician, make a joyful sound on your instrument today for the Lord! Encourage others that you know to do the same thing. Rejoice in the gift of music!

June 11

> *Sing* to him a new song; play skillfully, and shout for joy. (Psalm 33:3; emphasis mine)

This is such an inspirational verse for every person who has written something for God. The creativity comes from Him! The Holy Spirit inspires us to write and to play! There is a feeling one gets when playing something new for someone else that is incredibly satisfying. The person who gets to hear something new for the very first time can also be blessed! Praise God for every new song!

June 12

> I will turn my ear to a proverb; with the *harp* I will expound my riddle. (Psalm 49:4; emphasis mine)

What a powerful picture! Have your Bible open to Proverbs and play music to enhance the verses of Scripture. Think about that for a minute. Listening or playing music the same time you are in Proverbs, or to Psalms, since most of them are songs.

June 13

> For the director of *music*. According to gittith. Of the Sons of Korah. A psalm. How lovely is your dwelling place, lord Almighty! (Psalm 84:1; emphasis mine)

The gittith is a musical instrument, mentioned three times in the Psalms, and would have a unique sound. The song "How Lovely Is Your Dwelling Place" would be beautiful on any stringed instrument. Songs that reflect on heaven are special. Praise God today that He is going there to prepare a place for us! How great will the music be in heaven?

June 14

> And I saw what looked like a sea of glass glowing with fire and, standing beside the sea, those who had been victorious over the beast and its image and over the number of its name. They held *harps* given them by God. (Revelation 15:2; emphasis mine)

God will personally hand out the harps! What an image that creates. The victory is ours! We have overcome the beast, and we will get to rejoice playing music! How great would the sound of thousands of harps played in unison be? Praise God for music!

June 15

> Moses replied: "It is not the sound of victory, it is not the sound of defeat; it is the sound of *singing* that I hear." (Exodus 32:18; emphasis mine)

Don't you just love to hear a large group of people singing? Especially if it is one of your favorites! Every song that we sing to God is a favorite of His. Let people hear you sing today! Praise God for all the singers that you know, especially the little ones.

June 16

> The birds of the sky nest by the waters;
> they *sing* among the branches. (Psalm 104:12;
> emphasis mine)

I hope you are reading this early in the morning and you are being blessed by hearing the birds praise God by singing to Him. Not only does God create so many varieties of birds, He gives them their own sounds, their own language that only they understand. Praise God today for the birds and the fact that they sing to Him. So should we!

June 17

> Let the wilderness and its towns raise
> their voices; let the settlements where Kedar
> lives rejoice. Let the people of Sela *sing* for joy;
> let them shout from the mountaintops. (Isaiah
> 42:11; emphasis mine)

Singing for joy! Shouting from the mountaintops! At the start of the day, as we prayerfully praise God for all He has done, with our hearts and our minds being ready for whatever the day's assignment is. Then at the end of the day, knowing that what we accomplished was because God allowed it should give us reason again to sing for joy and shout from the mountaintops!

June 18

> [The Festival of Trumpets] On the first day
> of the seventh month hold a sacred assembly and
> do no regular work. It is a day for you to sound
> the *trumpets*. (Numbers 29:1; emphasis mine)

Notice that blowing the trumpet was not considered work! It was an opportunity to serve and to bring glory to God! When we have the opportunity to play our instruments or to sing for Him before an assembly, let's praise and thank Him for that privilege. Praise God for the trumpet players you know!

June 19

> So, Gideon sent the rest of the Israelites home but kept the three hundred, who took over the provisions and *trumpets* of the others. Now the camp of Midian lay below him in the valley. (Judges 7:8; emphasis mine)

From 32,000 men, the Lord reduced the size of the army that Gideon was to lead to only 300. Part of the 300 men included those who play trumpet! Of course, the Lord wanted to make sure that Gideon and the men who were going into battle knew that the victory was already in hand because of the word of the Lord. The Lord is also there for your battle. Blow the trumpet and move forward!

June 20

> The *musicians*: the descendants of Asaph 128, all children of Asaph. (Ezra 2:41; emphasis mine)

What a family reunion that would be—128 musicians in one family, all blessed with musical talent. Some certainly were vocalists. Praise God for all the musicians and vocalists in your immediate family and your extended family.

June 21

> For the director of *music*. A psalm of David. When the prophet Nathan came to him after David had committed adultery with Bathsheba. Have mercy on me, O God, according to your unfailing love; according to your great compassion blot out my transgressions. (Psalm 51:1; emphasis mine)

One of the songs that has been written based on this psalm is "Create in Me a Clean Heart." There is a great message to all of us here to acknowledge when we sin! We have a sinful nature, and the enemy looks for opportunities to trip us up. Confess it to God. Even sing it to Him.

June 22

> May the nations be glad and *sing* for joy,
> for you rule the peoples with equity and guide
> the nations of the earth. (Psalm 67:4; emphasis
> mine)

At one time, the United States was a Christian nation where God was honored and revered. Songs of worship, praise, and thanksgiving were written and were sung in churches on Sundays. It is God who established the great country of the USA. It is the population that has been deceived by the enemy that now wants God out of the country. Pray we can sing again about our country turning back to God.

June 23

> Then the woman went to all the people
> with her wise advice, and they cut off the head
> of Sheba son of Bikri and threw it to Joab. So,
> he sounded the *trumpet*, and his men dispersed
> from the city, each returning to his home. And
> Joab went back to the king in Jerusalem. (2
> Samuel 20:22; emphasis mine)

Trumpets were used in all kinds of situations, especially ones of significance. Here, the head of Sheba, who was an enemy of King David, was cut off. The mission had been accomplished, so the trumpet was sounded. Play your instrument after every accomplishment. Play it for God!

June 24

> God is with us; he is our leader. His priests
> with their *trumpets* will sound the battle cry
> against you. People of Israel, do not fight against
> the lord, the God of your ancestors, for you will
> not succeed. (2 Chronicles 13:12; emphasis
> mine)

Whose priests? God's! Who is the leader? God! We know that trumpets are used to signal when really important events are going to happen or have happened. Praise God for the pastors in your life, the service men and women in your life, and the trumpet players!

June 25

> For the director of *music*. According to gittith. A psalm of David. lord, our Lord, how majestic is your name in all the earth! You have set your glory in the heavens. (Psalm 8:1; emphasis mine)

This is the first of three times that the musical instrument called a gittith is mentioned in the Psalms. The wonderful worship songs that have been inspired by this verse! Has the Lord inspired you today? Play something for the Lord! Look at His glory and be inspired!

June 26

> For the director of *music*. A psalm of David. Hear me, my God, as I voice my complaint; protect my life from the threat of the enemy. (Psalm 64:1; emphasis mine)

How powerful is music? God encourages us to ask Him for anything and everything, even in song! There is no complaint or problem that is off-limits to God. We are invited to share our lives with Him, as David did, even when it appears that things are not going the way we want. Sing to Him!

June 27

> With *trumpets* and the blast of the ram's horn—shout for joy before the lord, the King. (Psalm 98:6; emphasis mine)

Praise God for the sounds of trumpets! For ram's horns! Praise Him that He loves to hear us sing and shout for joy over something that He has enabled us to accomplish! Praise God today for any and every accomplishment that you have done, from the smallest to the greatest. Sing and shout praise to Him!

June 28

> They have blown the *trumpet*, they have
> made all things ready, but no one will go into
> battle, for my wrath is on the whole crowd.
> (Ezekiel 7:14; emphasis mine)

Is it possible to play in an inappropriate time? Play in the wrong circumstance? If God is not ready to move forward, we should not attempt to. The trumpet was sounded, but God was not pleased. Always prayerfully consider when and where to play and if God has anointed the time and place.

June 29

> May they *sing* of the ways of the lord,
> for the glory of the lord is great. (Psalm 138:5;
> emphasis mine)

Singing! Using the voice that God blessed you with for His glory! Are the ways of the Lord, outlined in Scripture, a part of your ways? Sing for those ways! Do you see the glory of God in your life? Look out your window at dawn or at sunset, visual displays of God's glory. Sing to Him!

June 30

> A day of *trumpet* and battle cry against
> the fortified cities and against the corner towers.
> (Zephaniah 1:16; emphasis mine)

This is one event that you would never want to be a part of! This is prophecy of the judgment coming on the whole earth on the day of the Lord. Everything—man, beast, and every living thing— will be destroyed. The trumpet sound that we will hear will be at the rapture, when we will be united with the Lord.

July 1

> Now David was clothed in a robe of
> fine linen, as were all the Levites who were
> carrying the ark, and as were the musicians, and
> Kenaniah, who was in charge of the *singing* of
> the choirs. David also wore a linen ephod. (1
> Chronicles 15:27; emphasis mine)

If you have ever sung in a formal choir, you have been given a robe to wear. It is a garment that designates you as one of a special group. In this case, all the musicians were clothed in robes of fine linen as well. Dressing in a special garment makes you feel wonderful. Dress up in something special today and play your instrument! Sing out loud to the Lord!

July 2

> Shout aloud and *sing* for joy, people of
> Zion, for great is the Holy One of Israel among
> you. (Isaiah 12:6; emphasis mine)

What is the shouting all about? What is the song about? The musicians are happy about what? It is the Lord God, the Holy One of Israel! Our relationship with Him should cause us to shout aloud, "Thank You!" and sing praises to Him. Someday we will do that in person with Jesus! Practice it today!

July 3

> And, moreover, that the Gentiles might
> glorify God for his mercy. As it is written:
> "Therefore I will praise you among the Gentiles;
> I will *sing* the praises of your name." (Romans
> 15:9; emphasis mine)

Can you imagine? Jesus, your Lord and Savior, singing praises about you! When Jesus said to "love the Lord your God with all your heart, and with all your soul, and with all your mind and with all your strength," He also has loved you with all His heart, soul, mind, and strength. Love the Lord today!

July 4

> *Sing* to God, *sing* in praise of his name, extol him who rides on the clouds; rejoice before him—his name is the lord. (Psalm 68:4; emphasis mine)

Every day should be a day of celebration of our freedom. Today as Americans, we celebrate the founding of this country. Millions of dollars are spent on fireworks that are visible for only a few seconds. Let's make sure we do not short our tithe to fund the work of the kingdom for something that lasts only a few seconds. Rejoice in the celebration!

July 5

> The *musicians* also were brought together from the region around Jerusalem—from the villages of the Netophathites. (Nehemiah 12:28; emphasis mine)

> The sound of an exceptionally large praise team! Exhilarating and inspiring! Worship music to bring glory to God in abundance! Praise God for your praise team, for Christian concerts, and for the musicians that you know personally. Thank them for serving.

July 6

> For the director of *music*. Of David the servant of the lord. I have a message from God in my heart concerning the sinfulness of the wicked: There is no fear of God before their eyes. (Psalm 36:1; emphasis mine)

Messages that are spoken through music can be even more powerful than just talking. Having no fear of God is and will be tragic. Wide is the gate and broad is the road that leads to destruction, and many enter through it. Small is the gate and narrow the road that leads to life, and very few find it (Matthew 7:13–14).

July 7

> So, my heart laments for Moab like the *music* of a pipe; it laments like a pipe for the people of Kir Hareseth. The wealth they acquired is gone. (Jeremiah 48:36; emphasis mine)

A lament is a passionate expression of grief for someone, as Jeremiah was expressing here for Moab and the people of Kir Hareseth. The sound of the pipe as an instrument touched a special place in Jeremiah's heart. Is there an instrument sound that draws you closer to God? Praise Him for music!

July 8

> *Sing* the praises of the lord, enthroned in Zion; proclaim among the nations what he has done. (Psalm 9:11; emphasis mine)

Songs that bring glory to the Lord for what He has done seem to be timeless. "Amazing Grace," "How Great Thou Art," and "The Old Rugged Cross" are examples of worship songs proclaiming what He has done for us. These are songs that we can sing before all nations. Sing to Him today!

July 9

> After that you will go to Gibeah of God, where there is a Philistine outpost. As you approach the town, you will meet a procession of prophets coming down from the high place with lyres, timbrels, pipes and *harps* being played before them, and they will be prophesying. (1 Samuel 10:5; emphasis mine)

Saul is about to have his life changed dramatically. Samuel has just given him direction and has advised him that the power of the Lord will come upon him. Notice the opening event here, with music as the background for the prophets. What a great sound that would have been! Praise God for the musicians you know that play guitars, harps, and flutes!

July 10

> The *musicians* Heman, Asaph and Ethan were to sound the bronze cymbals. (1 Chronicles 15:19; emphasis mine)

A special mention here for percussionists. Bronze cymbals would have had a unique sound. No matter what you play, work at it with all your heart; even when learning a new instrument, it is symphonic when it reaches the Lord's ears. Praise God for our drummers!

July 11

> Awake, my soul! Awake, *harp* and lyre! I will awaken the dawn. (Psalm 57:8; emphasis mine)

First thing in the morning! Spending time with the Lord is great anytime, but at daybreak, it is special. Awake, my guitar! Awake, my harp! Let us make music to the Lord. It is the Holy Spirit that is driving that desire for music and to bring glory to God. Praise God for music!

July 12

> Satisfy us in the morning with your unfailing love, that we may *sing* for joy and be glad all our days. (Psalm 90:14; emphasis mine)

Waking up to that feeling of being blessed by the Lord and full of thanksgiving for all that He has provided is so wonderful. Sing praise to God in appreciation for His protection and provision for you. He is our shepherd, our comforter, and our all in all. Sing to Him!

July 13

> On the morning of the third day there was thunder and lightning, with a thick cloud over the mountain, and a very loud *trumpet* blast. Everyone in the camp trembled. (Exodus 19:16; emphasis mine)

The Lord God is going to meet with Moses on Mount Sinai, with all of Israel present. The sound of the trumpet was the signal to everyone that it was time. The blast (from heaven) was so loud that everyone trembled. Praise God for our trumpet players!

July 14

> Moses sent them into battle, a thousand from each tribe, along with Phinehas son of Eleazar, the priest, who took with him articles from the sanctuary and the *trumpets* for signaling. (Numbers 31:6; emphasis mine)

The sound that every person was familiar with, the blast from the trumpet, one of God's favorite instruments. It is used in music and as the signal that something especially important was about to happen. When Jesus comes back, there will be another trumpet call. Praise God if you are anxiously awaiting that call!

July 15

> As they began to *sing* and praise, the lord set ambushes against the men of Ammon and Moab and Mount Seir who were invading Judah, and they were defeated. (2 Chronicles 20:22; emphasis mine)

Think about that for a moment. How powerful it is when we sing to the Lord. As soon as they began, the Lord put their victory in motion. Praise God today by singing to Him and praying for the victory that you need. Let Him put His plan into action in response to your praise!

July 16

> *Sing* for joy, you heavens, for the lord has done this; shout aloud, you earth beneath. Burst into song, you mountains, you forests and all your trees, for the lord has redeemed Jacob, he displays his glory in Israel. (Isaiah 44:23; emphasis mine)

Ever feel like you could just explode with joy? Isaiah expresses this in a wonderful word picture from the heavens to the trees on the mountains. Ever see a sunrise or a sunset that took your breath away? The Lord has redeemed Jacob, displaying His glory in Israel. Sing for joy today! Praise God for all that you see!

July 17

> For the director of *music*. A maskil of David. When Doeg the Edomite had gone to Saul and told him: "David has gone to the house of Ahimelek." Why do you boast of evil, you mighty hero? Why do you boast all day long, you who are a disgrace in the eyes of God? (Psalm 52:1; emphasis mine)

All the psalms are, in effect, songs. I would be curious to know what the music director would do with this. A *maskil* is defined as "a person versed in Hebrew or Yiddish literature." Saul had become a disgrace to God, seeking to kill David, a man after God's own heart.

July 18

> Dividing the three hundred men into three companies, he placed *trumpets* and empty jars in the hands of all of them, with torches inside. (Judges 7:16; emphasis mine)

From thirty thousand to just three hundred men, God intended to display the power of faith and obedience. Gideon did as the Lord had commanded him, and after having been advised that the victory was theirs, he placed trumpets and glass jars into the hands of his army. At the right moment, the trumpets were sounded, and the jars were broken, and the Lord caused the Midianites to turn on themselves. Praise God for trumpet players!

July 19

> I will *sing* to the lord all my life; I will *sing* praise to my God as long as I live. (Psalm 104:33; emphasis mine)

Musicians and vocalists all agree that singing and playing music for the Lord is the most rewarding performances of all. The Lord blesses those who serve in music, and that feeling is totally satisfying. Our souls become filled with the righteousness of God and gives us the desire to sing praises to Him all the days of our lives. Praise God today for the gifts and talents He blessed you with.

July 20

> The priests, the Levites, the *musicians*, the gatekeepers and the temple servants settled in their own towns, along with some of the other people, and the rest of the Israelites settled in their towns. (Ezra 2:70; emphasis mine)

As a musician, you are in a special class of people. You are blessed with a gift that is to be used to glorify God by serving in His kingdom. Praise God for music-based assignments! No matter what you do, work at it with all your heart, as though working for the Lord, not just for men.

July 21

> There have Zadok the priest and Nathan the prophet anoint him king over Israel. Blow the *trumpet* and shout, "Long live King Solomon!" (1 Kings 1:34; emphasis mine)

All significant events in Scripture are heralded by the sound of the trumpet, a favorite instrument of God. In this case, David's son

Solomon is to be anointed as king. Praise God for all the trumpet players that you know.

July 22

> For God is the King of all the earth; *sing* to him a psalm of praise. (Psalm 47:7; emphasis mine)

God created you with a gift to be able to play and sing music. This is a great psalm of instruction for us: sing a song of praise to God! Whether the Holy Spirit is inspiring you to write something new or to play something that sounds great on your instrument, play and sing for God! He loves to hear you!

July 23

> Judah turned and saw that they were being attacked at both front and rear. Then they cried out to the lord. The priests blew their *trumpets*. (2 Chronicles 13:14; emphasis mine)

Abijah and his army of four hundred thousand defeated Jeroboam and his army of eight hundred thousand because God took control of the situation. The priests blew their trumpets, and God responded. Incredible how God can use a musical instrument to announce that He is about to change the world. There will be a trumpet call when Jesus returns, and this world will be changed. Praise God for the trumpet call!

July 24

> All you people of the world, you who live on the earth, when a banner is raised on the mountains, you will see it, and when a *trumpet* sounds, you will hear it. (Isaiah 18:3; emphasis mine)

The unmistakable sound of the trumpet, God says all will hear it. "When the trumpet of the Lord shall sound and time shall be no more, and the morning breaks eternal bright and fair; when the saved of earth shall gather over on the other shore and when the roll is called up yonder, I'll be there."

July 25

> For the director of *music*. To the tune of "The Death of the Son." A psalm of David. I will give thanks to you, lord, with all my heart; I will tell of all your wonderful deeds. (Psalm 9:1; emphasis mine)

Not sure what the melody of "The Death of the Son" would sound like, but it certainly would not be a joyful song, yet David is intent on an attitude of thanksgiving. With all his heart, he wants to glorify God by singing and sharing what God has done. Can we praise God today for all He has done?

July 26

> For the director of *music*. A psalm of David. A song. Praise awaits you, our God, in Zion; to you our vows will be fulfilled. (Psalm 65:1; emphasis mine)

A great way to praise God is to sing to Him. Fulfill the vows that you have made to Him and rejoice in the opportunity to sing to Him. He loves to hear your voice and delights in hearing you play your instrument. Praise God today for all the musicians and vocalists you know. Encourage each one!

July 27

> And he sees the sword coming against the land and blows the *trumpet* to warn the people. (Ezekiel 33:3; emphasis mine)

One thing for certain is that when you hear the sound of the trumpet, it gets your attention immediately. There is no mistake about what you heard. No wonder God chose this instrument to announce important events. Praise God for the trumpet players in your life!

July 28

[*The* lord *Will Appear*] Then the lord will appear over them; his arrow will flash like lightning. The Sovereign lord will sound the *trumpet*; he will march in the storms of the south. (Zechariah 9:14; emphasis mine)

The Lord Himself will sound the trumpet! The enemies of Israel will be destroyed. The prophecy in this Old Testament book also mentions Jesus's entry into Jerusalem on a donkey. Imagine the majestic sound of a heavenly trumpet. Praise God for all the horn players!

July 29

I will *sing* a new song to you, my God; on the ten-stringed lyre I will make music to you. (Psalm 144:9; emphasis mine)

The twelve-string guitar is very close to the ten-string lyre. There are ten strings with individual notes, and two strings are duplicated, for a total of twelve. The sound is very full and rich. Praise God for the guitars that are used to create and play music. Praise God for the guitar players that you know.

July 30

And I saw the seven angels who stand before God, and seven *trumpets* were given to them. (Revelation 8:2; emphasis mine)

Seven angels chosen by God for incredible assignments. As each one sounded their trumpet, God's wrath began to pour out on the earth. Devastating judgment! Praise God that for all who have accepted Jesus as personal Lord and Savior, as we will not watch this in person. The trumpet is used by God to initiate His sovereign will.

July 31

For the director of *music*. Of the Sons of Korah. A psalm. You, lord, showed favor to your

land; you restored the fortunes of Jacob. (Psalm
85:1; emphasis mine)

Music to praise God for being restored. Something taken down
and then rebuilt. Something taken away and then retrieved. Something
withheld and then released. Sing to God! Praise Him for being delivered,
for being restored, for being renewed. Praise Him for the love that He
has shown us.

August 1

> Then Jehoiada placed the oversight of the temple of the lord in the hands of the Levitical priests, to whom David had made assignments in the temple, to present the burnt offerings of the lord as written in the Law of Moses, with rejoicing and *singing*, as David had ordered. (2 Chronicles 23:18; emphasis mine)

Structured worship, there is some benefit to that. Plenty of room for rejoicing and singing during the burnt offerings. Praise God for the musicians and singers who led the nation in rejoicing! The next time you grill outside, rejoice and sing to the Lord! Whatever you are cooking was created by Him!

August 2

> All the lands are at rest and at peace; they break into *singing*. (Isaiah 14:7; emphasis mine)

When your soul is at peace, singing comes easily. The apostle Paul reflects that a "peace of God that transcends all understanding" is a result of prayer. Praise God today for the peace that only He can provide, not temporary but sustained. Sing to Him!

August 3

> So, what shall I do? I will pray with my spirit, but I will also pray with my understanding; I will *sing* with my spirit, but I will also *sing* with my understanding. (1 Corinthians 14:15; emphasis mine)

Knowing Jesus gives us access to the Father. Praying with the understanding that Jesus created that access. Sing with that understanding! Your spirit yearns for that joy! The Holy Spirit rejoices in hearing you pray and sing!

August 4

> God sets the lonely in families, he leads out
> the prisoners with *singing*; but the rebellious live
> in a sun-scorched land. (Psalm 68:6; emphasis
> mine)

God cares about widows, orphans, and those who are in prison, deserving or not. He leads with singing! We have also learned that He sounds a trumpet at significant events. Praise God if you have been adopted or comforted in the loss of a spouse and if you are now free from prison. Sing to Him!

August 5

> From Beth Gilgal, and from the area of
> Geba and Azmaveth, for the *musicians* had
> built villages for themselves around Jerusalem.
> (Nehemiah 12:29; emphasis mine)

The musicians were sought out to come to the dedication of the wall that was rebuilt in Jerusalem. An incredible time for celebration! The wall was done! God never lets talent go to waste! This was a victory in the face of adversity for Israel. Praise God for your victories! Sing to Him!

August 6

> For the director of *music*. For Jeduthun.
> A psalm of David. I said, "I will watch my
> ways and keep my tongue from sin; I will put
> a muzzle on my mouth while in the presence of
> the wicked." (Psalm 39:1; emphasis mine)

A unique prayer to put to music! A great prayer request and great advice. Putting some of the hardest things to say into music makes the

...

message sweeter. Pray for the opportunities to sing about wisdom and obedience for the Lord! Make a joyful noise for Him!

August 7

> The elders are gone from the city gate;
> the young men have stopped their *music*.
> (Lamentations 5:14; emphasis mine)

Can you imagine a day with no music? Something that God Himself loves to hear. For a situation to become so drastic that the musicians have stopped their music would just be horrible. Pray that you never are in circumstances that would justify having no music to praise God.

August 8

> Besides their 7,337 male and female slaves;
> and they also had 245 male and female *singers*.
> (Nehemiah 7:67; emphasis mine)

What a choir that would be! The full range of voices from soprano to bass and all levels of alto and tenor. What range do you sing in? Praise God for vocalists! Praise God for the music that drives the singing!

August 9

> David and all Israel were celebrating with
> all their might before the lord, with castanets,
> *harps*, lyres, timbrels, sistrums and cymbals. (2
> Samuel 6:5; emphasis mine)

Sistrums are from ancient Egypt and are in the percussion family, as are castanets. These would have added musical flavor to the guitars and harps. The tambourines and cymbals would have provided meter. Praise God for the musicians that play these types of instruments!

August 10

> Four thousand are to be gatekeepers and
> four thousand are to praise the lord with the
> *musical* instruments I have provided for that
> purpose. (1 Chronicles 23:5; emphasis mine)

Four thousand musicians! All with musical instruments provided by the Lord! What a great assignment! Praise God for those that have been blessed with a special talent to play an instrument that brings glory to Him! Praise God for the assignments that God gives to use that gift. Play for Him!

August 11

> Awake, *harp* and lyre! I will awaken the
> dawn. (Psalm 108:2; emphasis mine)

Praise God for those times of inspiration when you cannot wait for the beautiful colors of the dawn and the freshness of a new day for the opportunity to bring the musical instrument that you play to life! The sound of the instrument is controlled by the musician. The musician, controlled by God, is great!

August 12

> For you make me glad by your deeds, lord;
> I *sing* for joy at what your hands have done.
> (Psalm 92:4)

I will enter His gates with thanksgiving and His courts with praise (Psalm 100:4)! Praise God for the things He has done in your life, the evidence of His omniscience. Sing for joy about the blessings you have because of His care and love for you. Sing to Him!

August 13

> As the sound of the *trumpet* grew louder
> and louder, Moses spoke, and the voice of God
> answered him. (Exodus 19:19; emphasis mine)

Moses has led the people of Israel to Mount Sinai. The blast from the trumpet was so loud that the people trembled with fear. God always uses the trumpet to signify an important event. Praise God today for the trumpet players that you know! There is a spot in heaven's praise team for them!

August 14

> Have seven priests carry *trumpets* of rams' horns in front of the ark. On the seventh day, march around the city seven times, with the priests blowing the *trumpets*. (Joshua 6:4; emphasis mine)

Trumpets made from rams' horns, not from metal, are known as shofars. They create a different sound. The number of priests and the assignment was orchestrated by God. Seven times around the city, blowing the trumpets all the way. Praise God for the trumpet players!

August 15

> But the servants of Achish said to him, "Isn't this David, the king of the land? Isn't he the one they *sing* about in their dances: 'Saul has slain his thousands, and David his tens of thousands'?" (1 Samuel 21:11; emphasis mine)

Victories are certainly worth singing about! In this case, the vocalists were dancing while they were singing. Praise God for the freedom of expression! We can sing and dance for His glory. We can rejoice in the victories He provides for us!

August 16

> The lord will surely comfort Zion and will look with compassion on all her ruins; he will make her deserts like Eden, her wastelands like the garden of the lord. Joy and gladness will be found in her, thanksgiving and the sound of *singing*. (Isaiah 51:3; emphasis mine)

The joy of restoration inspires the soul to sing! The sounds of musical instruments playing in harmony with one another, filling the air with beautiful sound. Vocalists of every range singing songs that bring glory to the Lord, full of thanksgiving for what He has done. Sing to Him!

August 17

> For the director of *music*. According to Mahalath. A maskil of David. The fool says in his heart, "There is no God." They are corrupt, and their ways are vile; there is no one who does good. (Psalm 53:1; emphasis mine)

Maskil is used thirteen times in Psalms and is a person versed in Hebrew or Yiddish. In this case, Mahalath would have been the follower of David. What a song to be written! I wonder if this would have been one of the early blues tunes. A sad description of the fool.

August 18

> When I and all who are with me blow our *trumpets*, then from all around the camp blow yours and shout, "For the lord and for Gideon." (Judges 7:18; emphasis mine)

The sound that all the warriors were familiar with, the sound of the trumpet. As in most instances, the trumpet was used to signify an important event. In this case, the call to battle as God gives Gideon's army of three hundred men the victory of tens of thousands of their enemies. Blow your trumpet today!

August 19

> *Sing* to him, *sing* praise to him; tell of all his wonderful acts. (Psalm 105:2; emphasis mine)

Love the instructions given to us in this verse of Scripture: Sing to the Lord! Sing praises to Him! Sing about the wonderful things He has accomplished. Songs such as "Bless the Lord," "Amazing Grace/ My Chains Are Gone," "There Is a Fountain" are some great ones to sing. Let Him hear your voice today!

August 20

> Some of the Israelites, including priests, Levites, *musicians*, gatekeepers and temple servants, also came up to Jerusalem in the seventh year of King Artaxerxes. (Ezra 7:7; emphasis mine)

The four-month journey from Babylon to Jerusalem was funded by the king for Ezra and the company of Israelites to return home. What a privilege to be allowed to be included in that group. As a musician, you would have joyfully sung and played to encourage others on the journey. Praise God for musicians!

August 21

> Zadok the priest took the horn of oil from the sacred tent and anointed Solomon. Then they sounded the *trumpet* and all the people shouted, "Long live King Solomon!" (1 Kings 1:39; emphasis mine)

The reign of King Solomon, the wisest, richest king in history, begins. The trumpet heralded the initiation, and a feast began. All the people were shouting praise to Solomon. Praise God today for His sovereign rule, His omniscience, and that He is still in control.

August 22

> Deliver me from the guilt of bloodshed, O God, you who are God my Savior, and my tongue will *sing* of your righteousness. (Psalm 51:14; emphasis mine)

A plea for forgiveness, a prayer for God to cleanse David. The blood shed was Uriah's, Bathsheba's husband. Nathan, the prophet, exposes the cover-up by David, and he is broken in his repentance. He does know that God's forgiveness will allow him to sing to God. Sing to God today. Praise Him for forgiving you.

August 23

> They took an oath to the lord with loud
> acclamation, with shouting and with *trumpets*
> and horns. (2 Chronicles 15:14; emphasis mine)

With loud and enthusiastic approval, they took an oath to the Lord, shouting and with the horn section in the background. Have you taken an oath to God? Have you made a vow to Him? Consider what the Lord may be asking of you and then commit to it! Approve of it! Sing to Him!

August 24

> And in that day a great *trumpet* will sound.
> Those who were perishing in Assyria and those
> who were exiled in Egypt will come and worship
> the lord on the holy mountain in Jerusalem.
> (Isaiah 27:13; emphasis mine)

The Lord will gather them one by one, and they will worship Him. Someday there will be another trumpet sound, and all of us that have accepted Jesus Christ as our personal Lord and Savior will be caught up to meet Him in the air! Sing to Him about that day! "When the Roll Is Called Up Yonder!"

August 25

> For the director of *music*. A song. A psalm.
> Shout for joy to God, all the earth! (Psalm 66:1;
> emphasis mine)

The song "Your Presence" has a line: "I take refuge in the shadow of your wings, close to you is where I want to be." Are you in the care of the Savior? Could you flee anywhere that would not be in His presence? Praise God for His love for you! Sing to Him!

August 26

> For the director of *music*. Of David. In
> the lord I take refuge. How then can you say to

me: "Flee like a bird to your mountain." (Psalm 11:1; emphasis mine)

Ever hear the "Victory Chant"? Hail, Jesus, You're my King! Hail, hail, Lion of Judah! Sing to the Lord today! Shout out something to the Lord that you love about Him. Find a favorite worship song and sing it loud! If you play an instrument, play it for an audience of one: Jesus.

August 27

> Then if anyone hears the *trumpet* but does not heed the warning and the sword comes and takes their life, their blood will be on their own head. (Ezekiel 33:4; emphasis mine)

All throughout the history of Israel, the Lord used the trumpet as His instrument of choice to herald an event of great magnitude. Every generation would have been familiar with that process. Here, the warning in prophecy is crystal clear: obey or die. Choose to obey!

August 28

> So, when you give to the needy, do not announce it with *trumpets*, as the hypocrites do in the synagogues and on the streets, to be honored by others. Truly I tell you, they have received their reward in full. (Matthew 6:2; emphasis mine)

Trumpets were always used to get attention, but when you are prayerfully serving the Lord, do not do anything that draws attention to your act of service. Colossians 3:23 says, "No matter what you do, work at it with all your heart as though working for the Lord, not just for men." Sing to Him, praise Him, be thankful for the opportunity to serve.

August 29

> They celebrate your abundant goodness and joyfully *sing* of your righteousness. (Psalm 145:7; emphasis mine)

The Lord is so good! The song "God Is So Good" reflects those feelings. Prayer and Scripture alone can be very inspiring. Serving in the kingdom is so rewarding that your heart can be full of joy! Being in fellowship with another brother or sister in Christ is special. Sing to Him!

August 30

> [The Trumpets] Then the seven angels who had the seven *trumpets* prepared to sound them. (Revelation 8:6; emphasis mine)

This was probably the most significant assignment for those seven angels. The trumpet is God's chosen instrument to signify that something important is about to happen. Here, the wrath of God is about to be poured out on the earth. Pretty significant for those that have not been caught up in the rapture.

August 31

> A song. A psalm of the Sons of Korah. For the director of *music*. According to mahalath leannoth. A maskil of Heman the Ezrahite. lord, you are the God who saves me; day and night I cry out to you. (Psalm 88:1; emphasis mine)

A special musical arrangement, acknowledging that it is God who saves us! Day and night He watches over us—our shepherd, our comforter, our all in all. Praise God today for the fact that He created you. There is not another person in the world like you. Praise Him for the gifts and talents He has blessed you with.

September 1

> Miriam sang to them: "*Sing* to the lord,
> for he is highly exalted. Both horse and driver
> he has hurled into the sea." (Exodus 15:21;
> emphasis mine)

Can you imagine? Walking between two walls of water as though on dry ground. Then, after approximately two million people get on the other side, here comes the pharaoh's army. The walls of water collapse in on them. Horse and rider are drowned. How could you not sing!

September 2

> Joy and gladness are taken away from the
> orchards; no one *sings* or shouts in the vineyards;
> no one treads out wine at the presses, for I have
> put an end to the shouting. (Isaiah 16:10;
> emphasis mine)

When the Lord has had enough, the good times come to an end. Encourage the musicians and singers that you know to always play and sing as if for an audience of one, the Lord. To be the best musician and singer that you can be requires obedience in all areas so that God is glorified.

September 3

> Speaking to one another with psalms,
> hymns, and songs from the Spirit. *Sing* and make
> music from your heart to the Lord. (Ephesians
> 5:19; emphasis mine)

What a great way to encourage one person or a group! Sing something, play something, and with an attitude of pleasing the Lord.

Remember, He wants the glory for the gifts and talents that He has blessed you with. Sing from your heart! Sing for Him!

September 4

> In front are the *singers*, after them the musicians; with them are the young women playing the timbrels. (Psalm 68:25; emphasis mine)

The procession begins with the singers, with the musicians providing the background music right behind them. The young women are adding some percussion with tambourines. What an incredible parade of talent orchestrated by God. The music would have inspired the whole nation.

September 5

> And his associates—Shemaiah, Azarel, Milalai, Gilalai, Maai, Nethanel, Judah and Hanani—with *musical* instruments prescribed by David the man of God. Ezra the teacher of the Law led the procession. (Nehemiah 12:36; emphasis mine)

There were many musicians, but in this case only a few are mentioned by name. One thing is for sure, God has your name, and next to it is the talent that He blessed you with. Next to that is a record of every time you have sung and played to bring glory to Him. Sing for Him! Play for Him!

September 6

> For the director of *music*. Of David. A psalm. I waited patiently for the lord; he turned to me and heard my cry. (Psalm 40:1; emphasis mine)

There are seventeen verses in this psalm. Each could be written as a verse in the song, with a chorus of "Great is the Lord!" Are you writing anything for the Lord? Be sure it includes praise for all He has done! Praises first, then prayer requests. Sing something new for Him!

September 7

> I will put an end to your noisy songs, and
> the *music* of your harps will be heard no more.
> (Ezekiel 26:13; emphasis mine)

Just like any parent, sometimes enough is enough. There was more than once when the Lord said to Israel, "Enough!" It is not just the ability to play and sing well, the rest of our lives have to display an obedience that glorifies God. Encourage one another to be in prayer and Scripture and in fellowship with other Christians.

September 8

> I will *sing* the lord's praise, for he has been
> good to me. (Psalm 13:6; emphasis mine)

Do you know the song "God is so good, God is so good, God is so good, He's so good to me"? There are three to four verses to this simple tune, but praise is at the heart of it. Take the time to praise and thank God every day for His provision for you. Sing your appreciation to Him!

September 9

> A psalm. A song. For the Sabbath day. It is
> good to praise the lord and make *music* to your
> name, O Most High. (Psalm 92:1; emphasis
> mine)

Every Sunday service in our church starts with worship music. It is a call to put our attention on Him, to prepare our hearts to be open to hear the message that He has prepared the pastor to deliver. As a musician, making music for the Lord is the most satisfying project we will ever do!

September 10

> All these men were under the supervision
> of their father for the *music* of the temple of
> the lord, with cymbals, lyres and harps, for the

ministry at the house of God. Asaph, Jeduthun and Heman were under the supervision of the king. (1 Chronicles 25:6; emphasis mine)

Praise God for the exceptionally talented musicians. There are a multitude of guitar players, but only a few are truly exceptional. The same goes for every instrument. Not that all are not talented, they are. Some have been blessed in a special way. Praise God for those musicians you know that are above and beyond the average players and singers.

September 11

"But now bring me a *harpist*." While the *harpist* was playing, the hand of the lord came on Elisha. (2 Kings 3:15; emphasis mine)

The kings of Israel, Judah, and Edom are about to take on Moab, but they need water. They call on Elisha, who was with Elijah and was known to be a man of God. Elisha asked for a harpist. While the harp was played, the Lord was with Elisha, and he prophesied about water and victory. Praise God for harp players.

September 12

Come, let us *sing* for joy to the lord; let us shout aloud to the Rock of our salvation. (Psalm 95:1; emphasis mine)

A call to worship! The song "Come, Now Is the Time to Worship" comes to mind. Let us sing for joy to Jesus, our Rock, our Redeemer, our Savior! One thing happens when you shout; you put your whole self into that moment. Shout some praise to the Lord! Sing to Him!

September 13

There on the poplars we hung our *harps*. (Psalm 137:2; emphasis mine)

A poplar tree is not the ideal music stand, but it is what was available. Praise God for the music cases that have been designed specifically for each instrument. Thank Him that we have a place to rest our instruments during breaks. Praise Him for all the musicians that you know!

September 14

> When the people saw the thunder and lightning and heard the *trumpet* and saw the mountain in smoke, they trembled with fear. They stayed at a distance. (Exodus 20:18; emphasis mine)

Not only did the nation hear God's trumpet, but they also saw the and heard the thunder and lightning amid the smoke on Mount Sinai. How do we hear the voice of God? By reading Scripture. The next time you see and hear a thunderstorm, take a minute and praise God for the majestic power He displays.

September 15

> Hezekiah gave the order to sacrifice the burnt offering on the altar. As the offering began, *singing* to the lord began also, accompanied by trumpets and the instruments of David king of Israel. (2 Chronicles 29:27; emphasis mine)

Praise God that because of Jesus, our sin debt is paid! Even though there is no longer a need to sacrifice an animal on Sunday, the music is just as important. Singing to the Lord is something we will do throughout eternity! Praise God for His provision, Jesus, the Lamb of God who took away our sin!

September 16

> When you hear them sound a long blast on the trumpets, have the whole army give a loud shout; then the wall of the city will collapse and the army will go up, everyone straight in. (Joshua 6:5; emphasis mine)

The Lord required obedience from Joshua and the Israeli army, to not do anything other than use the trumpets in the manner He designed them for and to shout! The Lord took the walls down and gave the victory to Joshua. Let us be obedient in the little things God has for us.

September 17

> A song. A psalm of David. My heart, O God, is steadfast; I will *sing* and make music with all my soul. (Psalm 108:1)

Being full of the Spirit is such a wonderful, satisfying feeling. These are the moments of great creativity. Pick up that instrument that God blessed you with the ability to play and sing for Him a new song! Write what is on your heart, being grateful, being thankful, and for being loved. Sing for Him!

September 18

> Those the lord has rescued will return. They will enter Zion with *singing*; everlasting joy will crown their heads. Gladness and joy will overtake them, and sorrow and sighing will flee away. (Isaiah 51:11; emphasis mine)

Oh, the joy of being restored! The delight in getting to return home again. When we are full of joy, that becomes a crown for us. When we get to be with Jesus, oh, what joy will be ours. Singing praises to God will be normal and not a burden. Sing for Him!

September 19

> For the director of *music*. With stringed instruments. A maskil of David. When the Ziphites had gone to Saul and said, "Is not David hiding among us?" Save me, O God, by your name; vindicate me by your might. (Psalm 54:1; emphasis mine)

What a song this must have been! David in hiding from Saul and the Ziphites turning him in. David knew what we should know—that God is in control. No matter the outcome on earth, you have been vindicated in heaven. God will deal with those who have wronged you. Vengeance is His!

September 20

> You are also to know that you have no authority to impose taxes, tribute or duty on any of the priests, Levites, *musicians*, gatekeepers, temple servants or other workers at this house of God. (Ezra 7:24; emphasis mine)

Being a musician puts you in a special class. Either playing an instrument or being a vocalist is a gift from God. Bring glory to Him today by playing your instrument or by singing some of your favorite songs and hymns. Do you know that He loves to hear you? Sing and play for Him!

September 21

> Gideon and the hundred men with him reached the edge of the camp at the beginning of the middle watch, just after they had changed the guard. They blew their *trumpets* and broke the jars that were in their hands. (Judges 7:19; emphasis mine)

It was an orchestrated attack designed by God and followed by an obedient Gideon. The trumpets were sounded just after midnight, and the rout was on. Let us be obedient in rehearsing our music. Let us be diligent practicing in playing and singing. Let us bring glory to the Lord in all we do.

September 22

> My heart, O God, is steadfast, my heart is steadfast; I will *sing* and make music. (Psalm 57:7; emphasis mine)

What is in your heart today? That is what matters to your heavenly Father. More than what we do is the why we do it. Being unwavering and resolute in our commitment to music for Him will be a blessing. To be steadfast in our desire to use the gifts He has blessed us with for His glory. Bearing fruit!

September 23

> Adonijah and all the guests who were with him heard it as they were finishing their feast. On hearing the sound of the *trumpet*, Joab asked, "What's the meaning of all the noise in the city?" (1 Kings 1:41; emphasis mine)

Adonijah had a very short-lived term as a self-appointed king to follow David. When the trumpet was sounded in the celebration of Solomon being anointed, Joab wanted to know what was happening. I think the Lord made the sound especially loud in Adonijah's ears, as he was out of order. Praise God today for the sounds of your instrument, and especially the trumpet.

September 24

> So, the Levites stood ready with David's instruments, and the priests with their *trumpets*. (2 Chronicles 29:26; emphasis mine)

The burnt offering is lit, and the song to the Lord commences with the trumpets. Then the musicians with cymbals and harps and lyres accompany the singers. The celebration and worship are under way! Praise God for the variety of sounds that He has created and the gifted musicians to play them.

September 25

> For the director of *music*. According to sheminith. A psalm of David. Help, lord, for no one is faithful anymore; those who are loyal have vanished from the human race. (Psalm 12:1; emphasis mine)

This verse could almost be a headline in today's paper. The definition of *sheminith* is as confusing as any term in our modern language. It could have been an instrument or a reference to the eighth note on the scale, which would be an octave of the first note. The content suggests a blues tune. Sing anyway!

September 26

> For the director of *music*. With stringed instruments. A psalm. A song. May God be gracious to us and bless us and make his face shine on us. (Psalm 67:1; emphasis mine)

Maranatha singers sang a song during the Promise Keepers' era entitled "Stretch Out Your Hand." The verse follows the title with, "And heal this nation. Stretch our your hand, and bring restoration. Let your mercy overflow us, like a never-failing stream, by the blood of Jesus cleanse us, O Lord it's you we seek, cause your face to shine, upon us again." What a great prayer request.

September 27

> [True Fasting] Shout it aloud, do not hold back. Raise your voice like a *trumpet*. Declare to my people their rebellion and to the descendants of Jacob their sins. (Isaiah 58:1; emphasis mine)

Be loud! Be loud like the sound of the trumpet! Be purpose driven in your commitment to God. If we need to repent of something, let's do it with all our heart. Confess to God with a sincerity that is complete, with a heart that is broken. God loves to pick us up and move forward.

September 28

> Since they heard the sound of the *trumpet* but did not heed the warning, their blood will be on their own head. If they had heeded the warning, they would have saved themselves. (Ezekiel 33:5; emphasis mine)

There is a reason that God established the trumpet as His preferred instrument of warning. Every generation would have been familiar with the sound and its meaning. Not heeding the warning has serious consequences. His word is like a silent trumpet. Let's listen to what He says in it.

September 29

> I will praise the lord all my life; I will *sing* praise to my God as long as I live. (Psalm 146:2; emphasis mine)

When we are filled with the Spirit, having spent time in prayer, in Scripture, and in fellowship with other believers, we are so blessed that we never want that feeling to end. Singing praise to God is something we can do up until our last breath. Sing for Him today.

September 30

> And he will send his angels with a loud *trumpet* call, and they will gather his elect from the four winds, from one end of the heavens to the other. (Matthew 24:31; emphasis mine)

The most beautiful-sounding trumpet ever! The call to come home to the place Jesus went to prepare for us so that we may be with Him. Are you ready? The day will come when we will be caught up to meet Him in the air, and our adventures in eternity will begin! Sing and play to Him today!

October 1

> Therefore, I will praise you, lord, among
> the nations; I will *sing* the praises of your name.
> (Psalm 18:49; emphasis mine)

Not only in my house, not only in my city, my state, and my country but in other nations as well, I will sing praises to You for who You are and what You have done. The greatest of these is paying a sin debt that we could never pay! Eternal life in heaven is a free gift! How can we not sing!

October 2

> Take up a harp, walk through the city,
> you forgotten prostitute; play the harp well, *sing*
> many a song, so that you will be remembered.
> (Isaiah 23:16; emphasis mine)

Tyre was a city that the Lord was about to destroy, and the prophet Isaiah was issuing the warning of what was to come. For seventy years, Tyre would be no more. The reference to the harp and to the singing which will be the only remnant.

October 3

> Let the message of Christ dwell among
> you richly as you teach and admonish one
> another with all wisdom through psalms,
> hymns, and songs from the Spirit, *singing* to
> God with gratitude in your hearts. (Colossians
> 3:16; emphasis mine)

Fellowship with other Christians is the best! Church is fine, but getting to know one another in a small group is the best. Even better when singing and music are incorporated into the meeting. Sometimes a song can have a deeper influence than just words alone. Powerful! Sing to Him!

October 4

> *Sing* to the lord a new song; *sing* to the lord, all the earth. (Psalm 96:1; emphasis mine)

Love the inspiring word of the Lord. Write and sing something new to Him; let the Holy Spirit touch your heart. As a musician, discovering a new way to express praise to God is exciting. Sharing something that the Lord has given you is a way to fill your soul with love for Him.

October 5

> They performed the service of their God and the service of purification, as did also the *musicians* and gatekeepers, according to the commands of David and his son Solomon. (Nehemiah 12:45; emphasis mine)

Serving the Lord as a musician is wonderful. Whether you play an instrument or you are a vocalist, having the opportunity to serve using the gifts and talents He gave you is truly a blessing. Praise God for every worship set that you have been a part of. Sing for Him!

October 6

> For the director of *music*. A psalm of David. Blessed are those who have regard for the weak; the lord delivers them in times of trouble. (Psalm 41:1; emphasis mine)

The Lord says that every time we provide food, water, clothing, a place to stay, or visit someone sick or in prison, it is the same as doing it for Him! Praise God for every song that centers our attention around serving others. Sing a praise to God for the opportunities He shows you.

October 7

> As soon as you hear the sound of the horn, flute, zither, lyre, harp, pipe and all kinds of *music*, you must fall down and worship the image of gold that King Nebuchadnezzar has set up. (Daniel 3:5; emphasis mine)

Sometimes, the gift of being a musician can be used in the wrong way. In fact, if the music does not bring glory to God, it is wrong. Praise God that we know what is right and what is wrong. We can make musical choices that honor our Lord. Be strong in the Lord! Sing and play for Him!

October 8

> I will praise you, Lord, among the nations; I will *sing* of you among the peoples. (Psalm 57:9; emphasis mine)

At every opportunity that the Lord provides for you to play and to sing, rejoice! He has a plan for your gift. He wants you to bless those that He put on your path specifically for what you play. You may be an encouragement to someone who wants to play. Be ready for those assignments to play!

October 9

> David and all the Israelites were celebrating with all their might before God, with songs and with *harps*, lyres, timbrels, cymbals and trumpets. (1 Chronicles 13:8; emphasis mine)

What a concert! Not just a little get-together but the whole nation! Not just barely singing but singing and playing with all their might! Colossians 3:23 says, "No matter what you do, work at it with all your heart as though working for the Lord, not just for men." What a feeling to play with all your heart for Him!

October 10

> Along with their relatives—all of them trained and skilled in *music* for the lord—they numbered 288. (1 Chronicles 25:7; emphasis mine)

How about that for a praise team! All of them trained and skilled in music. Musicians and vocalists all in unison, all wanting to worship the Lord. What an incredible sound it must have been. What an incredible sound the music in heaven will be! For now, play to Him with all your heart, soul, mind, and strength!

October 11

> Praise him with the sounding of the trumpet, praise him with the *harp* and lyre. (Psalm 150:3; emphasis mine)

Stringed instruments and wind instruments sound really good together. The modern-day harp has forty-seven strings! Also, it has seven pedals to raise or lower the pitch. A twelve-string guitar adds lots of depth to the chords being played. All sound great with horns, trumpets, flutes, and saxophones! Play for Him!

October 12

> To the *music* of the ten-stringed lyre and the melody of the harp. (Psalm 92:3; emphasis mine)

Even though there are only seven major keys, have octaves to each of those strings add quite a nice touch to the music. The twelvestring modern guitar has ten individual-sounding strings, with two strings being duplicated. The harp is one of the most heavenly sounding instruments ever created. Play for Him!

October 13

> Say to the Israelites: "On the first day of the seventh month you are to have a day of

sabbath rest, a sacred assembly commemorated with *trumpet* blasts." (Leviticus 23:24; emphasis mine)

A day of rest, except for the trumpet players. What a privilege to have an assignment that was so important that your instrument was used on the Sabbath. Can you play something to commemorate a special day for the Lord? Of course you can! Play and sing for Him!

October 14

Let the trees of the forest *sing*, let them *sing* for joy before the lord, for he comes to judge the earth. (1 Chronicles 16:33; emphasis mine)

The breeze, created by God, is like the maestro of the forest orchestra. The leaves make certain sounds when the breeze blows through them. Larger leaves, smaller leaves, all in harmony with their Creator. Are you in harmony with your Lord and Savior Jesus? With your heart right, play for Him!

October 15

I am now eighty years old. Can I tell the difference between what is enjoyable and what is not? Can your servant taste what he eats and drinks? Can I still hear the voices of male and female *singers*? Why should your servant be an added burden to my lord the king? (2 Samuel 19:35; emphasis mine)

Praying that no matter how old the Lord has destined you to be, you will be able to sing and play for Him. That you will be able to enjoy the voices of male and female singers! That you will be able to distinguish keys and what is in tune. Pray for the older musicians that you know.

October 16

> "*Sing*, barren woman, you who never bore a child; burst into song, shout for joy, you who were never in labor; because more are the children of the desolate woman than of her who has a husband," says the lord. (Isaiah 54:1; emphasis mine)

Regardless of your situation, one request from the Lord is constant: sing! Praise God for the things you have and the things He has done! Praise God for the child that God has put on your path, whether the child is yours or not. Love them as the Lord loves you. Sing to that child. Sing about God!

October 17

> For the director of *music*. With stringed instruments. A maskil of David. Listen to my prayer, O God, do not ignore my plea. (Psalm 55:1; emphasis mine)

David is in the middle of making a plea to God. Pleas are urgent and emotional requests. The chords used by the music director for this song were probably major keys and boldly struck. Maybe with a more subtle bridge for emphasis. Music helps deliver the message. Praise God for music!

October 18

> So Joshua son of Nun called the priests and said to them, "Take up the ark of the covenant of the lord and have seven priests carry *trumpets* in front of it." (Joshua 6:6; emphasis mine)

For six days, the musicians only carried their trumpets in front of the ark, in front of the armed men as they marched around the city of Jericho. Then on the seventh day, they marched around the city seven times, but this time blowing their trumpets. Uniquely orchestrated by God Himself!

October 19

> All the earth bows down to you; they *sing*
> praise to you, they *sing* the praises of your name.
> (Psalm 66:4; emphasis mine)

All of creation has its own unique way of praising God! Each creation sings praises in the way designed by God. Praise God that He has created you and given you the ability to play or sing for Him. Sing praises to the Lord today, thanking Him for the opportunity. Sing for Him!

October 20

> From the *musicians*: Eliashib. From the
> gatekeepers: Shallum, Telem and Uri. (Ezra
> 10:24; emphasis mine)

Ever hope your name is not mentioned relative to breaking the law? The only musician found guilty was Eliashib. He had married a foreign woman, which Israelites were not allowed to do. Pray that your name and your reputation stay respected and God honoring. Play music with integrity. Play for Him!

October 21

> The three companies blew the *trumpets*
> and smashed the jars. Grasping the torches in
> their left hands and holding in their right hands
> the *trumpets* they were to blow, they shouted,
> "A sword for the lord and for Gideon!" (Judges
> 7:20; emphasis mine)

It is just after midnight, and the attack is now underway. God gave Gideon the battle plan. Notice it included one of God's favorite instruments, the trumpet! This instrument is used throughout Scripture as God's notice that something significant is about to happen. You are significant!

October 22

> They quickly took their cloaks and spread them under him on the bare steps. Then they blew the *trumpet* and shouted, "Jehu is king!" (2 Kings 9:13; emphasis mine)

An unexpected directive from the Lord! Jehu has been anointed king over Israel and has been ordered to destroy the house of Ahab, his master! The sound of the trumpet brings glory to God when it is used as He directs. Play your instrument as God has directed you, always to bring Him glory.

October 23

> When the builders laid the foundation of the temple of the lord, the priests in their vestments and with *trumpets*, and the Levites (the sons of Asaph) with cymbals, took their places to praise the lord, as prescribed by David king of Israel. (Ezra 3:10; emphasis mine)

Priests with trumpets and Levites with cymbals—it was an incredibly unique combination of instruments used in this celebration of the foundation of the temple being laid. Praying that prayer and Scripture are part of the foundation of your life, that your music abilities are celebrations of the gift that God gave you.

October 24

> [*Disaster From the North*] Announce in Judah and proclaim in Jerusalem and say: "Sound the *trumpet* throughout the land!" Cry aloud and say: "Gather together! Let us flee to the fortified cities!" (Jeremiah 4:5; emphasis mine)

God's judgment was coming, and the sound of the trumpet was used as the well-known sound that something was about to happen. Not a victory in this case, but a disaster was about to overtake them.

Someday the last trumpet will sound, and it will be glorious for some and disastrous for others.

October 25

> For the director of *music*. A psalm of David. How long, lord? Will you forget me forever? How long will you hide your face from me? (Psalm 13:1; emphasis mine)

What an encouragement for us! Even in some of the lowest points in David's life, he reaches out to his music director to put his anguished cry to music. This is surely a sad song! Ever had that feeling that God is upset with you? Put those feelings to music, into song. The birth of the blues!

October 26

> I will praise you, lord, among the nations;
> I will *sing* of you among the peoples. (Psalm 108:3; emphasis mine)

Especially for praise team members that look out at the congregation that God has called into your building for worship. When every range of people of brown from dark to light are singing and praising God together, with no boundaries on love, it is wonderful. Praise God for the power of music!

October 27

> For the director of *music*. Of David. A psalm. A song. May God arise, may his enemies be scattered; may his foes flee before him. (Psalm 68:1; emphasis mine)

Yes! David puts to music the encouraging request for God to arise! May His foes and enemies flee. David would report for duty to the Lord for any of these assignments. Are you available for an assignment from the Lord today? Can you sing and play a hymn of victory? How about "Battle Hymn of the Republic"?

October 28

> But if the watchman sees the sword coming
> and does not blow the *trumpet* to warn the people
> and the sword comes and takes someone's life,
> that person's life will be taken because of their
> sin, but I will hold the watchman accountable
> for their blood.' (Ezekiel 33:6; emphasis mine)

Sometimes the assignment of blowing the trumpet does not belong to a musician. In this instance, it was the responsibility of the watchman, whom God will hold accountable for not blowing it when he should. Does God use you and your instrument in important situations? Play and sing for Him!

October 29

> Again, if the *trumpet* does not sound
> a clear call, who will get ready for battle? (1
> Corinthians 14:8; emphasis mine)

Having the ability to play an instrument is a gift of God, but not everybody is gifted to play the same thing. Not everyone can blow a trumpet with the sound it is supposed to make. When you play your instrument, play it with all your heart, soul, mind, and strength, producing the right sounds.

October 30

> The first angel sounded his *trumpet*, and
> there came hail and fire mixed with blood, and
> it was hurled down on the earth. A third of the
> earth was burned up, a third of the trees were
> burned up, and all the green grass was burned
> up. (Revelation 8:7; emphasis mine)

The most significant trumpet sounds are documented in Revelation. Here the first of seven angels starts the process. The signal that some of the most incredible events in history are about to take place. Pray for everyone you know that they are not left behind to experience the wrath of God.

October 31

> Praise the lord. How good it is to *sing* praises to our God, how pleasant and fitting to praise him! (Psalm 147:1; emphasis mine)

When you serve the Lord, He gives your heart a hug. It is a warm satisfying feeling that nothing else can match. Singing to the Lord is such a blessing for the musician and for the audience. Praise God for the opportunities He gives you to play and sing for Him. Praise Him for the ability to share music!

November 1

> [*Contributions for Worship*] Hezekiah assigned the priests and Levites to divisions—each of them according to their duties as priests or Levites—to offer burnt offerings and fellowship offerings, to minister, to give thanks and to *sing* praises at the gates of the lord's dwelling. (2 Chronicles 31:2; emphasis mine)

A concert at the gates—not just any gates but gates to the Lord's dwelling! Praise God today for the greatest place you ever had the opportunity to praise Him. A stadium? A large auditorium? Even in a small room with first-time believers could be the greatest, depending on your heart. Sing for Him!

November 2

> From the ends of the earth we hear *singing*: "Glory to the Righteous One." But I said, "I waste away, I waste away! Woe to me! The treacherous betray! With treachery the treacherous betray!" (Isaiah 24:16; emphasis mine)

The Lord is going to destroy the earth, the peoples of the earth, and the heavens above the earth, yet a few will survive. The few who have been faithful will survive the last days. The few will be singing. "Small is the gate and narrow the road that leads to life, and very few find it" (Matthew 7:14).

November 3

> He says, "I will declare your name to my brothers and sisters; in the assembly I will *sing* your praises." (Hebrews 2:12; emphasis mine)

How about that! Jesus will sing your praises! Loving the Lord has included singing to Him on multiple occasions, singing His praises at every opportunity, and now when we get to be with Him, He will sing our praises. That is just incredible to think about. Play and sing for Him today with praises!

November 4

> *Sing* to the lord, praise his name; proclaim his salvation day after day. (Psalm 96:2; emphasis mine)

Jesus paid the price so that your soul can be with Him for eternity. He paid a sin debt that we could never pay. His gift of salvation to us was free! If we accept that gift and put our faith in Him as personal Lord and Savior, all we need to do is obey. Use the gifts and talents He gave you to glorify Him!

November 5

> For long ago, in the days of David and Asaph, there had been directors for the *musicians* and for the songs of praise and thanksgiving to God. (Nehemiah 12:46; emphasis mine)

God loves structure. Jesus tells us He is the vine, we are the branches, and our heavenly Father is the vinedresser. Having directors over music is structure. Song selection is a way to glorify God and bless the speaker giving the sermon. Praise God for your music director and your worship leader.

November 6

> For the director of *music*. A maskil of the Sons of Korah. As the deer pants for streams of water, so my soul pants for you, my God. (Psalm 42:1; emphasis mine)

Water sustains life for plants and animals as well as humans. There is a living water that Jesus provides that sustains our souls. We have such a need to be connected to God every moment of every minute of every day. Put your description of that need into words and sing it back to the Lord. Sing for Him!

November 7

> Let us come before him with thanksgiving
> and extol him with *music* and song. (Psalm 95:2;
> emphasis mine)

The song "Come, Now Is the Time to Worship," further, just as you are to worship Him. Singing praises to God, with thanksgiving in your heart, provides a spiritual blessing unmatched by anything else we can do. Music adds so much to the feelings being expressed in the verses. Play and sing for Him!

November 8

> Be exalted in your strength, lord; we
> will *sing* and praise your might. (Psalm 21:13;
> emphasis mine)

Nothing is impossible for the Lord. Consider every possible source of strength you have ever seen, and the Lord can surpass that. There is no power greater than His, no obstacle that He cannot handle, and nothing from the enemy can withstand His might. No one can snatch you out of His hand. Sing for Him!

November 9

> Therefore, as soon as they heard the sound
> of the horn, flute, zither, lyre, harp and all kinds
> of *music*, all the nations and peoples of every
> language fell down and worshiped the image
> of gold that King Nebuchadnezzar had set up.
> (Daniel 3:7; emphasis mine)

King Nebuchadnezzar is about to find out what a poor decision that was. But consider how powerful the music was in this situation. It inspired people, it encouraged people, it brought people together. It was for the wrong reasons, but still powerful. Play and sing for Him in all the right ways, for the right reasons. The gift He has blessed you with is to bring glory to Him!

November 10

> All the Levites who were *musicians*—Asaph, Heman, Jeduthun and their sons and relatives— stood on the east side of the altar, dressed in fine linen and playing cymbals, harps and lyres. They were accompanied by 120 priests sounding trumpets. (2 Chronicles 5:12; emphasis mine)

One of the few times we see that the musicians were dressed in choir-type robes or clothing. The orchestra included percussion, harps and guitars, and a horn section. What an incredible sound that would have been to hear. Praise God for every musician you know that plays one of these instruments.

November 11

> And Mattithiah, Eliphelehu, Mikneiah, Obed-Edom, Jeiel and Azaziah were to play the *harps*, directing according to sheminith. (1 Chronicles 15:21; emphasis mine)

These six musicians were part of a seventeen-member band put together and specifically sectioned by instrument. The structure is using lower octaves of keys for male voices. Praise God for His hand in structuring how you play, when you play, and where you are to serve, playing for Him.

November 12

> *Sing* to the lord with grateful praise; make music to our God on the harp. (Psalm 147:7; emphasis mine)

Sing for Him! A common theme throughout Scripture. God loves to hear you sing! Be grateful and full of thanksgiving. "I will enter His gates with thanksgiving in my heart, I will enter His courts with Praise" is a great verse in a great praise song. Make music on your instrument today. Play and sing for Him!

November 13

> They have *harps* and lyres at their banquets, pipes and timbrels and wine, but they have no regard for the deeds of the lord, no respect for the work of his hands. (Isaiah 5:12; emphasis mine)

Always know who you are being asked to play for. Where is the location? What is the event? Are you being asked to compromise your Christian values in any way? The enemy looks for opportunities to trap you into sinful behavior. Pray about any opportunity to play and sing that is outside of Christian paths.

November 14

> Then have the *trumpet* sounded everywhere on the tenth day of the seventh month; on the Day of Atonement sound the *trumpet* throughout your land. (Leviticus 25:9; emphasis mine)

The directive from God is clear. The assignment is unmistakable. The trumpet is the sound that gets attention. It became a familiar sound heralding something important has happened or will be happening. Praise God for the trumpet players in your life. Thank Him for their gift of music.

November 15

> But I will *sing* of your strength, in the morning I will *sing* of your love; for you are my fortress, my refuge in times of trouble. (Psalm 59:16; emphasis mine)

That is it! Because He is our refuge all the time, He is worthy to be praised all the time. Sing of what He has done for you! Sing about His word in your life. Sing about your prayer time with Him. Sing about the power of fellowship with other Christians! Sing and play for Him!

November 16

> My servants will *sing* out of the joy of
> their hearts, but you will cry out from anguish
> of heart and wail in brokenness of spirit. (Isaiah
> 65:14; emphasis mine)

What a contrast in attitudes. Those who love the Lord will sing out of the joy in their heart. Those who do not love the Lord will cry out from anguish and wail in brokenness of spirit. The enemy has deceived so many individuals into believing that there is no God, that Jesus is not the Lord. Believe in Jesus! Sing!

November 17

> For the director of *music*. To the tune of "A
> Dove on Distant Oaks." Of David. A miktam.
> When the Philistines had seized him in Gath.
> Be merciful to me, my God, for my enemies
> are in hot pursuit; all day long they press their
> attack. (Psalm 56:1; emphasis mine)

This is the only reference to this tune in Scripture. Considering his situation, I wonder what David had in mind for a melody. Have you ever been seized by your circumstances? Ever felt captive by life events? "Trust in the Lord with all your heart and lean not on your own understanding (Proverbs 3:5–6).

November 18

> When Joshua had spoken to the people,
> the seven priests carrying the seven *trumpets*
> before the lord went forward, blowing their
> *trumpets*, and the ark of the lord's covenant
> followed them. (Joshua 6:8; emphasis mine)

Seven is considered a complete number by many theologians. It is also the number of major keys in music. Here, seven priests carrying seven trumpets march around Jericho seven times. Underwritten in all this is the obedience to God's plans. He knows the plans He has for you! Sing for Him!

November 19

> When the three hundred *trumpets* sounded,
> the lord caused the men throughout the camp to
> turn on each other with their swords. The army
> fled to Beth Shittah toward Zererah as far as the
> border of Abel Meholah near Tabbath. (Judges
> 7:22; emphasis mine)

God is so good! On one occasion, He uses seven trumpets and a shout to collapse the walls of Jericho, then here He has Gideon's men blow their trumpets just after midnight. No wonder they turned on each other! God causes victories to happen in the most incredible ways. How can you not love Him!

November 20

> After the wall had been rebuilt and I
> had set the doors in place, the gatekeepers,
> the *musicians* and the Levites were appointed.
> (Nehemiah 7:1; emphasis mine)

Nehemiah led the charge to rebuild the walls of Jerusalem. Now he has put the worship structure back in place, including the musicians. The Levitical order was reestablished, and God was being properly praised again. Any walls in your heart that need to be rebuilt to protect you from the enemy?

November 21

> She looked and there the king,
> standing by the pillar, as the custom was. The
> officers and the *trumpeters* were beside the king,
> and all the people of the land were rejoicing and
> blowing *trumpets*. Then Athaliah tore her robes
> and called out, "Treason! Treason!" (2 Kings
> 11:14; emphasis mine)

Joash, at seven years old, has just been crowned king! Athaliah, a wicked woman, was put to death that day. No wonder the people were rejoicing and the trumpets were blowing. The next time someone you know that is worthy gets elected or appointed, play your instrument for them! Sing for Him!

November 22

> *Sing* to God, you kingdoms of the earth,
> *sing* praise to the Lord. (Psalm 68:32; emphasis mine)

The Lord loves to hear you sing! Sing about the freedoms you have, about all He has blessed you with. Sing about the gifts and talents He gave you. Sing about the worship music He has provided for you. Sing about the missionaries serving in other kingdoms that you support. Sing for Him!

November 23

> And each of the builders wore his sword at
> his side as he worked. But the man who sounded
> the trumpet stayed with me. (Nehemiah 4:18)

Not every musical instrument has been designated by God to be used in the manner of the trumpet. It was of supreme importance as it served as the notification, the alarm, the call to attention. Something was about to happen that God was involved in. Praise God for the trumpet players you know!

November 24

> Oh, my anguish, my anguish! I writhe
> in pain. Oh, the agony of my heart! My heart
> pounds within me, I cannot keep silent. For
> I have heard the sound of the *trumpet*; I have
> heard the battle cry. (Jeremiah 4:19; emphasis
> mine)

The sound of the trumpet announcing the oncoming onslaught! The Lord is devastating the land, annihilating people. The time had come when He had had enough. That time is coming soon. The Lord will destroy the earth and the heavens and will create a new heaven and a new earth. Then the only trumpet sounds will be on the praise teams!

November 25

> For the director of *music*. Of David. The
> fool says in his heart, "There is no God." They
> are corrupt, their deeds are vile; there is no one
> who does good. (Psalm 14:1; emphasis mine)

Another possible blues tune from David to the music director. How sad is it to know that many of the people in our world are fools and will left behind when the Lord comes back? They deny that there is a God, and that is proven by their deeds. Scripture is clear about how God feels regarding their deeds.

November 26

> Sound the *trumpet* in Gibeah, the horn in
> Ramah. Raise the battle cry in Beth Aven; lead
> on, Benjamin. (Hosea 5:8; emphasis mine)

Oh my goodness. This chapter in Scripture is as convicting as any about the behavior of God's people. They have turned away from Him, prostituted themselves to anything and everything that is detestable to God. Let our behavior bring glory to God in all we do. Let us bear fruit, showing ourselves to be His disciples.

November 27

> In front are the singers, after them the
> *musicians*; with them are the young women
> playing the timbrels. (Psalm 68:25; emphasis
> mine)

In many worship settings today, the setup is similar: singers in front of the musicians. The singers play such an important role in leading us in worship! Acapella is great, but music adds so much to the song. Musicians add powerful feelings to the words of praise we sing. Play and sing for Him!

November 28

> In a flash, in the twinkling of an eye, at
> the last *trumpet*. For the *trumpet* will sound, the
> dead will be raised imperishable, and we will be
> changed. (1 Corinthians 15:52; emphasis mine)

Are you ready? The last trumpet call is coming! A trumpet played by an angel of the Lord, specifically to those who belong to Him home. Home to our eternal home. The place Jesus said He was going to prepare for us. In the twinkling of an eye! Praise God for this promise! Sing praise to Him!

November 29

> May my tongue *sing* of your word, for all
> your commands are righteous. (Psalm 119:172;
> emphasis mine)

Psalm 119 has 176 verses. Around 158 of them contain one of six key words, of which *word* is one of them. Jesus said, "If you remain in me, and my words remain in you, ask whatever you wish, and it will be given you" (John 15:7). His word is so powerful! Sing a favorite verse to Him today!

November 30

> Why did you run off secretly and deceive
> me? Why didn't you tell me, so I could send
> you away with joy and *singing* to the music of
> timbrels and harps? (Genesis 31:27; emphasis
> mine)

Regardless of the situation, music enhances farewells and all kinds of celebrations. We do a lot of that today. Stringed instruments and tambourines make great sing-along music. Praise God for the opportunities you have to play a stringed instrument or tambourine. Play and sing for Him!

December 1

> Jeremiah composed laments for Josiah, and to this day all the male and female *singers* commemorate Josiah in the laments. These became a tradition in Israel and are written in the Laments. (2 Chronicles 35:25; emphasis mine)

Laments are passionate expressions of grief or sorrow. Jeremiah, the weeping prophet, composed verses of grief for Josiah, and all the singers learned these songs. Josiah was a great king but was killed in a battle that he was warned to stay out of. He was remembered for his obedience to the Lord. Will you be remembered for obedience? Jesus said, "If you love me, you will obey what I command."

December 2

> In that day—"*Sing* about a fruitful vineyard." (Isaiah 27:2; emphasis mine)

In John 15, Jesus says that He is the Vine and we are the branches. If we remain in Him and His words remain in us, we will bear much fruit, showing ourselves to be His disciples. Bringing glory to Him in what we do fills us with joy that we can sing about. Sing about being a fruitful disciple. Sing for Him!

December 3

> [The Prayer of Faith] Is anyone among you in trouble? Let them pray. Is anyone happy? Let them *sing* songs of praise. (James 5:13; emphasis mine)

Great instruction from the half brother of Jesus. Attitude is everything. Our attitude dictates our approach to the day, to the next assignment, and to the next person God puts on our path. Choose to be happy in Him! Rejoice in what you have. Praise Him in song for all He has done. Sing for Him!

December 4

> I will praise you with the harp for your faithfulness, my God; I will *sing* praise to you with the lyre, Holy One of Israel. (Psalm 71:22; emphasis mine)

Praise God that He is always there for us. He always wants the best for us and is ready to help us achieve His will in our lives. He has a purpose for each one of us and loves us all along our journey. Praise God for harp players and musicians that play guitars and lyres. Play and sing for Him!

December 5

> So, in the days of Zerubbabel and of Nehemiah, all Israel contributed the daily portions for the *musicians* and the gatekeepers. They also set aside the portion for the other Levites, and the Levites set aside the portion for the descendants of Aaron. (Nehemiah 12:47; emphasis mine)

As a musician, you would have been cared for on a daily basis. Your commitment to the Lord would have been to master your instrument, learn all the songs, and be ready to perform at any time. God still provides for His musicians and all His children. Trust Him! Play for Him!

December 6

> For the director of *music*. Of the Sons of Korah. A maskil. We have heard it with our ears, O God; our ancestors have told us what you did

in their days, in days long ago. (Psalm 44:1; emphasis mine)

One thing that God totally loves is for us to remember what He has done for us. Putting memories into song that praise Him is special. Music directors would have put musical arrangements together for words written and inspired by the Lord. A great assignment. Write something for Him today.

December 7

> Shout for joy to the lord, all the earth, burst into jubilant song with *music*. (Psalm 98:4; emphasis mine)

Since God created all the earth, it is fitting that all the earth should shout for joy! Sing jubilantly for the Lord! Praise your heavenly Father, the God of the universe, whom you have access to! How incredible is that? Jesus paid for your admission to the throne room of God. Sing to Him!

December 8

> Then my head will be exalted above the enemies who surround me; at his sacred tent I will sacrifice with shouts of joy; I will *sing* and make music to the lord. (Psalm 27:6; emphasis mine)

David is praising God for His total protection for him. We can do the same. Praise Him for His love for us, a love that has no boundaries. No one can snatch us out of our Father's hand. We should be willing to sacrifice anything He needs for the kingdom. Let us sing and make music to Him!

December 9

> Your Majesty has issued a decree that everyone who hears the sound of the horn, flute, zither, lyre, harp, pipe and all kinds of *music*

must fall down and worship the image of gold.
(Daniel 3:10; emphasis mine)

Even if the sound of the band was really good, following the decree was not an option for Shadrach, Meshach, and Abednego. They stayed faithful to God, even being thrown into a fiery furnace. Are you ready to stay faithful to God no matter the cost? Strengthen your relationship through prayer, Scripture, fellowship, and obedience no matter how good the world sounds.

December 10

The priests took their positions, as did the Levites with the lord's musical instruments, which King David had made for praising the lord and which were used when he gave thanks, saying, "His love endures forever." Opposite the Levites, the priests blew their trumpets, and all the Israelites were standing. (2 Chronicles 7:6)

What a worship service! The musicians, with their instruments, and the priests, with their trumpets, and all attending were standing, praising God because His love endures forever. Songs of rejoicing that bring glory to God such as "How Great Thou Art" comes to mind. Sing and play for Him today!

December 11

So, all Israel brought up the ark of the cov enant of the lord with shouts, with the sounding of rams' horns and trumpets, and of cymbals, and the playing of lyres and *harps*. (1 Chronicles 15:28; emphasis mine)

The ark was an important part of Israel's relationship with the Lord. Bringing the ark to the temple was a very big deal. The praise band had horns and trumpets, cymbals, and a string section of lyres and harps. A sound of rejoicing. Praise God for your opportunities to play or sing.

December 12

> Let the fields be jubilant, and everything
> in them; let all the trees of the forest *sing* for joy.
> (Psalm 96:12; emphasis mine)

Knowing the Lord, it is easy to understand that since He created everything and causes everything to grow, then everything should praise Him! Even the sound of the trees as the wind blows through is worshipful to Him. Worship the Lord today with your instrument and your voice!

December 13

> *Sing* to the lord! Give praise to the lord!
> He rescues the life of the needy from the hands
> of the wicked. (Jeremiah 20:13; emphasis mine)

Our God is a God of love, but there are things that He hates. Sinful, wicked behavior that causes harm to any of His chosen angers Him. Praise God that He loves us that much. Praise Him for boundaries that keep us from falling. Praise God for letting Jesus pay our sin debt. Praise Him for the Holy Spirit that helps us pray, helps us with direction, and is our lifeline. Praise God for His love for us.

December 14

> For the director of *music*. To the tune of
> "Do Not Destroy." Of David. A miktam. When
> he had fled from Saul into the cave. Have mercy
> on me, my God, have mercy on me, for in you
> I take refuge. I will take refuge in the shadow of
> your wings until the disaster has passed. (Psalm
> 57:1; emphasis mine)

Psalms 57, 58, 59, and 75 all start with David having the director of music put these songs to the tune of "Do Not Destroy." All the psalms are pleas for God's protection. In Him, we take refuge. The song "Leaning on the Everlasting Arms" comes to mind. Safe and secure from all alarms. Trust in the Lord today, for He is our refuge. Play and sing something for Him today, praising Him.

December 15

> Therefore, I will praise you, lord, among the nations; I will *sing* the praises of your name. (2 Samuel 22:50; emphasis mine)

Praying out loud adds to the sincerity of our praises and requests. Then when we add music to that, it becomes a song, and it is a new song. The Lord says, "Sing to Him a new song." Praise God today with your prayers, accompanied by the music you play. Play and sing for Him!

December 16

> All your pomp has been brought down to the grave, along with the noise of your *harps*; maggots are spread out beneath you and worms cover you. (Isaiah 14:11; emphasis mine)

Music that does not bring glory to the Lord is just noise to Him. Music that was once played for Him was being played for the one who betrayed Him. Now he has been brought down, and all who love the Lord rejoice at his falling. Praise God that He hears, and what He hears makes a difference to Him.

December 17

> Praise the lord. *Sing* to the lord a new song, his praise in the assembly of his faithful people. (Psalm 149:1; emphasis mine)

Getting together with other Christians to sing is always a wonderful time, especially during the Christmas season. Songs that stir our hearts and emotions as we praise our Lord and Savior. There is something new that happens when we sing one of the old hymns with someone or a group we have never sung with before. Sing for Him today! Invite someone to sing with you!

December 18

> Make two *trumpets* of hammered silver
> and use them for calling the community together
> and for having the camps set out. (Numbers
> 10:2; emphasis mine)

The only place in Scripture where silver is hammered into trumpets. The pattern was established, and the trumpet is one of God's favorite instruments. Someday, in the twinkling of an eye, there will be a trumpet call, and the community of believers in Jesus will be caught up with Him in the air! We will have truly set out for our new destination—heaven.

December 19

> The armed guard marched ahead of the
> priests who blew the *trumpets*, and the rear guard
> followed the ark. All this time the *trumpets* were
> sounding. (Joshua 6:9; emphasis mine)

What a sight (and sound) that would have been. Armed security marching in front, followed by trumpet-playing priests, followed by the ark, followed by more armed security. By the seventh day, I wonder if the inhabitants of Jericho were wondering if they would ever leave. Praise God that His battle plan included musicians. Have confidence in who God has called you to play for. He has a reason.

December 20

> The *musicians*: the descendants of Asaph
> 148. (Nehemiah 7:44; emphasis mine)

Nehemiah found a record listing those who were among the first to return to Jerusalem: 42,360 people. Among them, 148 musicians, the descendants of Asaph. When the books are opened in heaven, your name will be listed under *musicians*! Praise God for the gifts and talents He has blessed you with!

December 21

> Jonathan attacked the Philistine outpost at Geba, and the Philistines heard about it. Then Saul had the *trumpet* blown throughout the land and said, "Let the Hebrews hear!" (1 Samuel 13:3; emphasis mine)

Blow your trumpet today! Play for your King, Jesus. Let everyone know that Jesus has given you victory over the enemy. You have become a new creation; the old has gone. Play your instrument today with passion for the Lord. Let the world hear you play! Play and sing for Him!

December 22

> You are my strength, I *sing* praise to you; you, God, are my fortress, my God on whom I can rely. (Psalm 59:17; emphasis mine)

Every breath that you take is because God allowed it. He created you, designed you, and has a plan for you to bring glory to Him. Sing praise to God today. Sing about His mercy and grace to you. Your joy will have an impact on someone today. Sing about God's faithfulness. Sing to Him today!

December 23

> The money brought into the temple was not spent for making silver basins, wick trimmers, sprinkling bowls, *trumpets* or any other articles of gold or silver for the temple of the lord. (2 Kings 12:13; emphasis mine)

The money brought into the temple at this time was used to make repairs, maintenance that had been neglected for many years. It is great that at one time, kingdom funds were used to make trumpets! What will the instruments in heaven sound like? Play your instrument today with a desire to play for God in His temple. Play with all your heart!

December 24

> Wherever you hear the sound of the *trumpet*, join us there. (Nehemiah 4:20; emphasis mine)

The sound of the trumpet, heard throughout the land, is calling us to join others. This is a time of year when we should call others to join us. A time to celebrate the birth of our Lord Jesus. A time to share the story of how, when, and where Jesus came. Prophecy fulfilled! Our Savior! Sing about that today!

December 25

> Suddenly a great company of the heavenly host appeared with the angel, praising God and saying, "Glory to God in the highest heaven, and on earth peace to those on whom his favor rests." (Luke 2:13–14)

Songs for this time of year are incredibly powerful: "Angels We Have Heard on High," Silent Night," "O Little Town of Bethlehem," and so many more. Scripture comes to life through music! The song "The Little Drummer Boy" is an inspiration for all of us. Let us play our instrument for the King today!

December 26

> How long must I see the battle standard and hear the sound of the *trumpet*? (Jeremiah 4:21; emphasis mine)

Jesus tells us in John 16:33 that in this world we will have trouble, but that we should take heart because He has overcome the world! The sound of the trumpet calls us to join the battle. Sometimes practicing your instrument can be a battle. Find the time to play for Him today. Praise Him for that gift.

December 27

> For the director of *music*. To the tune of "Lilies." Of David. Save me, O God, for the waters have come up to my neck. (Psalm 69:1; emphasis mine)

This tune is mentioned three times in the Psalms. The melody would have become familiar, as the tune was used for separate occasions. In Psalm 45, is was a wedding song. In Psalm 69, it is a plea to be rescued, and in Psalm 80, it is to the Shepherd of Israel. Whatever the chord structure was, the tune was familiar. Many of our songs today are structured in a familiar pattern: verse, verse, chorus. Play something for the Lord today, something that you know by heart.

December 28

> [*Israel to Reap the Whirlwind*] Put the *trumpet* to your lips! An eagle is over the house of the lord because the people have broken my covenant and rebelled against my law. (Hosea 8:1; emphasis mine)

The alarm is being sounded! Israel's disobedience will now suffer the consequences! Let us not ever be in that position. Jesus said in John 14:15, "If you love me, you will obey my commands." Love the Lord today. Play and sing praises to Him for your salvation. Praise Him that Jesus paid for your sin.

December 29

> May your priests be clothed with your righteousness; may your faithful people *sing* for joy. (Psalm 132:9; emphasis mine)

May you always have the desire to bring glory to God every time you have the opportunity to sing and to play! He loves to hear you sing! He loves the time you spend in music. What a great way to express the love you have for God! Play and sing for Him today. Share the gift with some faithful people!

December 30

> For the Lord himself will come down
> from heaven, with a loud command, with the
> voice of the archangel and with the *trumpet* call
> of God, and the dead in Christ will rise first. (1
> Thessalonians 4:16; emphasis mine)

Love this verse! The trumpet call of God, played by an angel, calling us home! How fantastic this will be! The Lord Himself, in person, with a loud command! This is such an encouraging word! He is using the trumpet, not the harp or cymbals or any of the other instruments. For this special event, it is the trumpet! Praise God that He is coming back. Praise Him for the trumpet players that you know.

December 31

> The second angel sounded his *trumpet*, and
> something like a huge mountain, all ablaze, was
> thrown into the sea. A third of the sea turned
> into blood. (Revelation 8:8)

There are seven angels, each having a trumpet, and their assignment is announcing the wrath of God on the earth. The impact on those left behind on earth will be devastating. Those who have denied God access to their hearts will suffer as no one has ever suffered. Pray for those that God has put on your path. Pray that they will accept Jesus as personal Lord and Savior! Sing praise for Him!

ABOUT THE AUTHOR

Kevin Stout has been a musician for over fifty years and gave his life to Jesus twenty-nine years ago. Kevin is always inspired and encouraged by Scripture, so he wanted to use Jesus, his coauthor, to help him create a 365-day devotional that would encourage singers and musicians while sharing scripture.

www.ingramcontent.com/pod-product-compliance
Lightning Source LLC
Chambersburg PA
CBHW051214120626
46547CB00013B/1341